Healing EVANGELISM

Healing Evangelism

Strengthen Your Witnessing with Effective Prayer for the Sick

Don Dunkerley

Foreword by J. I. Packer

Chosen Books
A Division of Baker Book House Co
Grand Rapids, Michigan 49516

Published by Chosen Books
a division of Baker Book House Company
P.O. Box 6287, Grand Rapids, MI 49516-6287

Printed in the United States of America

Library of Congress Cataloging-in-Publication Data

Library of Congress-in-Publication Data

Dunkerley, Don.
Healing evangelism : strengthen your witnessing with effective prayer for the sick / Don Dunkerley.
p. cm.
Includes bibliographical references.
ISBN 0-8007-9227-0
1. Spiritual healing. 2. Prayer—Christianity. 3. Evangelistic work.
I. Title.
BT732.5.D86 1995
234'.13—dc 94-48424

Dedicated to my beloved brother

the **Rev. Peterson Sozi**

a minister in the Reformed Presbyterian Church
in Uganda
who helped me understand the relationship
between healing and evangelism

Contents

Part 5: Healing Evangelism in Different Settings

Part 6: Getting Started

Foreword

Whether special ministry for the healing of the unwell should be integrated into regular ministry of the Word of God, particularly in evangelism, has been a talking point among Christians ever since Pentecostal pioneers institutionalized this linkage in their preaching missions two generations ago. Some argue for the conjunction as restoring to the Church a dimension of the historic ministry of Jesus and His disciples. Others argue for it as providing powerful evidence that the God of the Gospel is real today. Clearly, when healings through prayer occur, whether privately or in public meetings (as sometimes they do, though sometimes they do not), both these contentions may reasonably be voiced, for as comments on what has happened they are true as far as they go.

But there is more to be said.

Don Dunkerley is a Presbyterian pastor-evangelist who comes at this question with a clear-headed theological concern. He wants first to establish a biblical perspective on the empirically proven fact that through his own ministrations, as through those of some others, God does on occasion heal sick bodies as well as sick souls. He then wants to recommend practice like his own, not as a gimmick but as a biblically warranted pattern of pastoral and evangelistic ministry that is appropriate and enriching anytime people are open to it.

At its deepest level, this is a book about prayer and divine sovereignty. It follows a path of insight that has not, I think, been set out quite like this before, one that seems to me more precisely biblical than some of the better-known alternatives. Let me explain.

Think first of evangelism. Evangelism means making known the Gospel of Jesus Christ in an invitatory way, calling on lost sinners to acknowledge that they have lived wrongly, to repent of doing so and to receive Christ as their Savior, Lord and Friend. This is a transforming transaction that, whatever its psychological complexities, occurs only through the sovereign grace of God in what is literally a new creation—that is, the perceptual and motivational change of heart, or inner being, that Jesus called new birth.

Scripture shows that there is a correlation, mysterious but real, between expectant prayer and this momentous event in people's lives. And it is a commonplace among Christians everywhere that evangelism, whether formal or informal, crowd-centered or one-on-one, needs to be soaked in prayer, or else we have no reason to expect it to prove fruitful. In bringing the lost to Himself, God uses persuasion as a means; and presenters of the Gospel must accordingly seek to persuade. But persuasion alone cannot change unregenerate hearts. Only God can do that, and He usually does it in connection with petitionary prayer.

Why is it that when prayer is made, conversions result? Not because petition for conversions has regenerative power in itself, nor because such prayer twists God's arm, inducing Him to do what He had not planned. The reason is that bringing sinners to faith through the Gospel message is one of the things God plans to do (ordinarily, at least) in a particular way—namely, in answer to prayers that He Himself prompts. Our petitions are an ordained link in the chain of His action; He suspends the doing of much that He purposes on people praying first. The biblical assurances that God will answer prayer made according to His will fit into this frame. We cannot predict how much difference such praying will make in any particular situation, but we can know that God, our loving Father, answers all His children's petitions in some sense positively, even though He may have to adjust the terms in which we make them. We can also know that we are always in God's will when we pray for fruit from the ministry of His Word.

This, then, is how the link between petitionary prayer and evangelistic fruitfulness should be understood.

Accordingly, when evangelistic communication is planned, wise Christians prepare for it with prayer. The communicators—preachers, writers, broadcasters and media people, counselors, purposeful gossipers of the Gospel and believers inviting family or friends to hear and read the Christian message—go first to God to ask His blessing on what they plan, and beg Him to bring folk to faith through their efforts. During the venture, and afterwards, too, they continue to pray that God will induce response to the communicated Word. In this they seek not their own glory but God's, and the good of those for whom they care. They pray expectantly and God answers effectively. Evangelism advances through prayer.

Now think of healing. Healing, whether of body or of mind (the two, of course, are bound up together), means feeling and functioning better than one did, with a prospect of staying that way. In everyday healing, treatment that counters whatever disturbed our physical and mental well-being combines with the spontaneous recuperative powers of the human system, which it is sometimes possible to reinforce. In the Bible, however, particularly in the recorded ministries of Jesus and His apostles, we meet many instances of supernatural healing through God's creative power, the power that brings about states of affairs that are inexplicable in terms of what went before. Indeed, we find in this category occasional resuscitations of corpses; but in light of the yet more staggering reality of Jesus' bodily resurrection this should hardly surprise us, and certainly should not present our faith with a problem, any more than the promise of our bodily reclothing on Resurrection Day should do. That God the Creator from time to time heals and renews human bodies, not only by prospering medical treatment but by creative touches yielding results beyond medical expectation or understanding, ought never to be in doubt. Nothing in this department is too hard for the Lord.

Until the mid-nineteenth century Christians knew that God sometimes heals supernaturally in answer to prayer, though this was not thought common. But such recorded instances as Luther praying Melanchthon back from death's door, and Richard Baxter's congregation praying away his tumor, raised no eyebrows and stirred no debate. More recently, however, unbalanced and heretical theologies of healing, cessationist counter-contentions ("no miracles in this age"), overblown expectations in some circles and the activities of charlatan "healing evangelists" (manipulative performers claiming in effect to be God's magicians) have made biblical sobriety on healing hard to come by, and have raised feelings of anger and hurt that render discussion difficult.

Don Dunkerley, by contrast, is low-key and hype-free in a most refreshing way. Dunkerley claims no personal gift of healing. He does not think Scripture entitles anyone to make such a claim. He promises healing to nobody. He knows that some who are prayed for will not be healed because God's plan for their good dictates otherwise. He does not say, as some on a guesswork basis do, that God wills to heal most of the invalids who are being prayed for, or to heal those He plans to heal immediately upon their being prayed for. He says only that as Jesus out of compassion healed as He preached, so we out of compassion should ask for a work of God on invalids' bodies just as we ask for a work on unbelievers' hearts, and that we are right to do this in contexts where the Gospel is being actively communicated. His leading thought is that as through expectant prayer people are saved who would not otherwise be saved, so through expectant prayer people are healed who would not otherwise be healed—for prayer is in both cases the ordained prerequisite of the blessing that is sought.

Here is sober wisdom, pastoral shrewdness, theological acumen, common sense and, I think, sound doctrine. Dunkerley's striking book deserves to be widely and sympathetically read.

—J. I. Packer

Part 1

Introduction to Healing Evangelism

Healing was a prominent part of the evangelism of Jesus Christ and His apostles, and it appears to be a major part of the success of many fast-growing churches and movements today.

But is healing by the power of Christ really for today? If so, how can it be done by evangelical Christians whose theology and style are not Pentecostal?

1

What Is Healing Evangelism?

The Christian woman did not tell her husband where she went on Sundays.

Idi Amin was then dictator of Uganda. His government was financed by Libya and Saudi Arabia because of his sincere promise to turn Uganda into a Muslim state by the mass murder of Christians. By conservative estimate, 500,000 persons were killed during his reign from 1971 to 1979. In a land of then eleven million, that was one out of every 22 men, women and children. Most churches were banned. All security forces had orders to search diligently for secret underground services and ask no questions but kill everyone. Even three persons found with a Bible represented a crime to be punished by firing squad in public execution.

The woman's husband was a member of the State Research Bureau, Amin's secret police. Every day he would tell her of his day's work: So many Christian services raided, so many Christians killed.

So she did not tell him that on Sundays she attended an illegal church pastored by the Rev. Peterson Sozi. The church met secretly in a garage in Kabowa, an out-of-the-way cluster of banana plantations off the Kampala-Entebbe Road.

One Sunday Peterson preached on Acts 3, which recounts the story of the lame man at the Beautiful Gate of the Temple. Peterson described how the apostle said to the lame man, "In the name of Jesus Christ of Nazareth, walk" (verse 6), and helped the man to his feet. Then that man began to walk and jump.

After the benediction, a twelve-year-old boy on crutches came up to Peterson and shook his hand.

"What was the sermon about?" Peterson asked, and then commanded, "In the name of Jesus Christ of Nazareth, walk."

He pulled the boy along, holding him by the hand, just as the apostle had helped the lame man up. The boy stumbled because he had never been able to walk. Suddenly he was walking, then running and jumping, holding his crutches in the air. The whole congregation regathered to praise the Lord for the miracle.

But that is not the end of the story. The boy had been brought to church by his mother, that same woman whose husband was a member of the State Research Bureau. And that Sunday she had to go home with a healed son.

"How come my son is walking?" her husband asked when they got home.

"I don't know," she said.

"My son has never been able to walk. Now he is running and jumping. You must know what happened. You must tell me."

"I can't."

"Why not?"

"Well, it's the people you're persecuting. They prayed for him and their God healed him."

"Where do these people meet?"

"I can't tell you. If you knew, you might do them some harm."

"How can I do them any harm? Their God healed my son. I want to go and thank their God."

"Do you promise you will do them no harm?"

"I promise."

"Do you promise you will tell none of your friends about them and where they meet?"

"I promise."

So they went to the garage, where the people were still praising God for the miracle. The father was so impressed, he could not keep his promise. He had to tell all his friends—in the secret police, the military police, the civil police and the Marines—that Jesus was performing miracles in a certain garage in Kabowa.

Soon many military men were coming to see for themselves and getting converted. Before long the congregation had a nucleus of born-again security men. They came wearing their uniforms and carrying their rifles, but they set down their rifles outside and went in and sat on the mats on the floor and became outlaws with the rest of the congregation. They were living double lives, soldiers of Amin and soldiers of Christ, the persecutors and the persecuted.

As time went on, when they heard that a certain church was to be raided, they would tell Peterson, who would tell the pastor, who would get word to the congregation that next Sunday they would meet in another place. When the soldiers arrived the next Sunday, no one was there.

The Kabowa congregation in the Amin years played a significant role in the history of the underground churches.

And it all began when a pastor had the faith to help a lame boy in the name of Jesus to walk.

Healing Evangelism Today

Using healing prayer in evangelism is a major emphasis in developing countries and is a reason for the meteoric rise of Pentecostal and charismatic churches in the twentieth century.

By healing prayer I mean two things:

1. Prayer ministry for those who are hurting physically, mentally or spiritually. This is direct, personal prayer, often accompanied by the laying on of hands and perhaps by anointing with oil.
2. Prayer that expects and often sees significant improvement (if not complete healing) by the power of the Holy Spirit, even as the prayer is being offered.

But not only Pentecostals and charismatics use healing in their evangelism. The Rev. Roger S. Greenway, a conservative Reformed missionary, wrote the following in the January 1993 edition of *Missionary Monthly*, a magazine for orthodox Calvinists:

> Jesus came preaching and healing. He commanded his disciples to do the same. Yet because of the excesses, counterfeits and unbiblical practices connected with "faith healing," many of us hesitate to bring up the subject of healing. We fear that some people will immediately label us as "Pentecostal."
>
> Missionaries observe that in many places the churches that grow most rapidly are churches that incorporate the ministry of healing into their normal church activities. This naturally raises questions about churches that downplay healing and also do not grow particularly well. Is there a correlation?

> Moreover, there are places where Christians cannot go to doctors or buy medicines, and healing in answer to prayer is the only hope the poor have. Among such people, it is important that missionaries avoid giving the impression that they have confidence only in hospitals, clinics, and medicines.
>
> Whether healings and other types of "signs and wonders" can be expected today, and whether healing should be actively sought through prayer, are some of the most talked about subjects in missions. In some countries, most of the breakthroughs among resistant people groups come as a result of, or in connection with, some kind of supernatural occurrence. . . .
>
> My advice to missionaries is to pray for the sick and distressed on every appropriate occasion. Pray for the healing of believers, and pray that unbelievers will be healed and saved.

Healing prayer is a key to growth in numbers of churches throughout the world. And using healing prayer as a means of evangelism is popular in churches around the world.

Healing Prayer in the World's Largest Church

"People who are hurting need people to pray for them." That is the basic assumption of the evangelism program of the Yoido Full Gospel Church in Seoul, South Korea.

I visited the church in 1990 to study its evangelistic program. I spent time with Lydia Swain, the personal assistant to the pastor, the Rev. David Yonggi Cho. I attended several services and visited the church's "Prayer Mountain"—a prayer retreat center on a mountain where three thousand people (ten thousand on weekends) are always praying. And I had dinner in the home of one of the Prayer Mountain pastors, the Rev. Youngbae Kim.

The only formal evangelistic program, I learned, is the church's network of weekly neighborhood prayer meetings or "cell groups." As a result of these prayer meetings, the church sees from ten thousand to eleven thousand new converts a month—almost all converts from paganism, Buddhism and shamanism, rather than crossovers from other Christian churches.

The prayer meetings open with the Apostles' Creed (recited at every service and meeting associated with the Yoido Church) and a Bible study of about fifteen minutes. Pastor Cho wishes the Bible study times were longer. But "our people love to pray," the Rev. Kim told me, explaining why the people move so quickly to prayer.

Everyone present is prayed for. One after another has the whole group gather around, lay hands on him or her and pray for any needs.

After that they pray for needs in the neighborhood. They may pray for a neighbor who is hospitalized, after which someone may say to the neighbor's husband, "I understand your wife is in the hospital."

"How did you know?" he asks.

"I'm in a group concerned about our neighborhood, and we've been praying for you and your wife. If you come to our meeting this week, we'll pray for you in person."

The neighbor comes and receives prayer for his wife. Each week he returns until, after several weeks, he becomes a Christian and joins the church.

In this way the Yoido Church has become the largest Christian church in history.

The effectiveness of this program is due not only to the congregation's love of prayer, but to their reputation for having a God who answers prayer and who often does so miraculously.

Healing Prayer in Glendale, California

Some time after my visit to Yoido, I visited First Presbyterian Church in Glendale, California. That church had studied the methods of the Yoido church and even had their own Prayer Mountain.

One Sunday evening I visited the prayer service in the church parlor, where weekly prayer teams gathered to pray for any who came. There was a good congregation the evening I was present. Some were prayer team members, some were seeking prayer. The service opened with praise songs and a brief devotional. Then they divided into small groups, each with a person needing prayer and a few prayer team members to lay hands on him or her, pray and perhaps anoint him or her with oil.

Since my visit the prayer team ministry has moved from the parlor on Sunday night to the sanctuary following the morning service, reflecting the congregation's growing acceptance of the healing ministry. The Glendale church is growing, with an evangelism program based on the thesis that "people who are hurting need people to pray for them." The people in Glendale, as those in Yoido, are finding that God answers prayer and often does so miraculously.

Some Personal Pointers

Here are some things I do in practicing healing evangelism:

- I pray to be sensitive to the Holy Spirit to know when there are persons I should pray for or when I should pray with special boldness and intensity. I also pray that power to heal will flow through me from the Lord.
- I look for opportunities to pray for people. While many people are offended if you speak to them about Christ, few are offended if you offer to pray for them.

- I often carry in my pocket a small vial of oil in case the Lord directs me to pray for someone in that way. A drop on the forehead is sufficient.
- When people ask me to pray for them, I try to take time with them. I touch them as I pray, when appropriate, at the point of pain.
- When I begin a time of prayer ministry with a person, recognizing that many physical ailments have spiritual causes, I pray silently to bind any spirits present that are not of Jesus and I ask the Holy Spirit for insight about how to pray.
- Because James wrote that physical problems often have spiritual roots and that confession of sin is often connected with prayer for healing (5:14–16), I encourage people to talk about spiritual problems that may be related to their physical need. I also seek insight from the Holy Spirit about any other spiritual causes.
- I expect, and often see, significant results. As I pray for people, they often testify that suddenly the pain is gone or other obvious symptoms are altered or reversed. As I pray, many testify that they feel heat being applied to the affected area. This is the healing power of the Holy Spirit.
- While instances of complete and instantaneous healing are rare, I often have the assurance that the healing process has begun or been significantly advanced in our prayer time, and I try to communicate that assurance.
- I look for opportunities at the conclusion of our prayer time to give a prophetic word of "strengthening, encouragement and comfort" (1 Corinthians 14:3).

Healing Evangelism through History

Healing and evangelism have been connected down through the centuries, going back to the example and instruction of Jesus Himself.

Christ's Evangelism

When Jesus evangelized, He

> went throughout Galilee, teaching in their synagogues, preaching the good news of the kingdom, and healing every disease and sickness among the people.
>
> Matthew 4:23

When He trained the Twelve to evangelize,

> he gave them power and authority to drive out all demons and to cure diseases, and he sent them out to preach the kingdom of God and to heal the sick.
>
> Luke 9:1–2

When He sent out 72 others to evangelize, He told them,

> Heal the sick who are there and tell them, "The kingdom of God is near you."
>
> Luke 10:9

The evangelism of Jesus Christ and His "associate evangelists" not only announced the nearness of the Kingdom of God but demonstrated its immanence and power by healing some persons and delivering others from evil spirits. Persons were snatched from the kingdom of Satan when they were delivered from his afflictions and torments. The kingdom of Satan was pushed back and the Kingdom of God advanced.

Jesus seemed to expect that this kind of evangelism would continue because He announced shortly before His ascension,

> These signs will accompany those who believe: In my name they will drive out demons; they will speak in new tongues; they will pick up snakes with their hands; and

> when they drink deadly poison, it will not hurt them at all; they will place their hands on sick people, and they will get well.
>
> Mark 16:17–18

In the Early Church

This evangelism did continue, at least through the book of Acts. The signs mentioned in Mark 16 are seen in Acts. The emphasis is not on supernatural deliverance from accidents or enemies—although Paul was delivered from an accidental snakebite and many more were rescued from those who wanted to harm them—but on healing from illness and deliverance from evil spirits. The Kingdom of God moved forward in demonstrable power.

There is significant historical evidence that the evangelism of the Church in the early centuries was likewise marked by frequent supernatural healings and deliverances.

Through the Reformation

In time, however, the faith and power of the Church grew weak. Reports of miraculous healings became increasingly infrequent. Before long the Church no longer believed that ordinary Christians had power from Jesus Christ to heal disease and drive out spirits. As these activities became rare, they were looked on as only for special "saints." Their use was no longer to demonstrate the power of the Kingdom of God but to authenticate the unique holy power of individual "saints."

Although the Reformation restored many elements of primitive Christianity, it did not restore an emphasis on supernatural healing in evangelism. This was not only because such healings were rare but because they were associated with Roman Catholic ideas of sainthood, which the Reformers rejected.

In Twentieth-Century Christendom

Many Christians today continue to believe that healing and deliverance should play no role in modern evangelism. This is due not to our loyalty to the Reformers but primarily to the influence of Western secular thought.

Humanism is like secondhand smoke: Because it is in the air around us, it is impossible to avoid being poisoned by it. Humanism causes us to feel, for example, that if there is no scientific explanation for something, it cannot have happened. Humanism also teaches us that nothing is real or significant that cannot be seen, felt, tasted or charged on our MasterCard.

Christians believe that God heals the sick, but only by scientific, nonsupernatural means. "Give wisdom to the doctors," we pray. "Guide the fingers of the surgeon. Cause the medicine to work." Rarely do we ask for miracles. And when we do, we do not usually expect them to occur.

Biblical Evangelism Restored

Nevertheless, there are in the twentieth century many movements to restore healing to its biblical role in evangelism. These efforts are found most commonly among less educated persons in Westernized countries and among persons in non-Western nations. Many movements began with persons whose education in the Western secular worldview is limited.

The first such effort was the Pentecostal movement, which began among uneducated African-Americans and whites of the "Appalachian diaspora" with a worldview unspoiled by the Enlightenment. The Pentecostal movement has spread rapidly worldwide, especially in developing nations. Theology that arose among the "hillbillies" is more easily transferable to nations in the developing world than the theology of ivory tower academics.

In more recent years the charismatic movement has spread belief in the gifts of the Holy Spirit to educated middle-class Americans and others. Charismatics often confess that their biggest problem has been a "paradigm shift" in which they had to reject their Western secular worldview and choose to accept the supernatural worldview of the Bible.

The Pentecostal and charismatic movements are advancing rapidly. Of all the church growth in the world today, ninety percent occurs among the twenty percent of Christians who are Pentecostal or charismatic. Although there were no Pentecostals or charismatics until the year 1900, there are, according to researcher David Barrett, 372 million today. One out of fourteen persons in the total world population is a Pentecostal or charismatic, and one out of five professing Christians.

A major factor in the growth of these movements is their emphasis on the power of Christ to heal and deliver. Their success demonstrates what Jesus and the apostles knew long ago: that people who are hurting need people to pray for them.

Pilgrimage

I could not have believed twenty-five years ago that I would write a book like this, because I did not accept—and, in some cases, strongly opposed—many of its teachings.

I was taught originally, in the social Gospel church in which I was reared and in the dispensational churches I attended after dispensationalists brought me to personal faith in Christ during my college years, that all miracles had ceased. Within a few years I became convinced that dispensationalism was a manmade system imposed on the

Bible, and after a time of study became a "five-point," Westminster Confession of Faith Calvinist (which I still am). I identified with the neo-Puritan movement and befriended some of its leaders, including D. Martyn Lloyd-Jones, Iain Murray and J. I. Packer, who has been very helpful to me in my pilgrimage.

Belief that the gifts and miraculous power of the Holy Spirit are for today is almost as rare in neo-Puritan circles as it is in dispensationalist.

During my seminary years I had a negative experience with fellow students in a neo-Pentecostal prayer group—one of the seeds from which the later charismatic movement grew. In the years following, as I watched the movement arise, I transferred my hostility against the prayer group to the whole movement.

A major turning point in my thinking was a conversation I had with Dr. Lloyd-Jones in the summer of 1972. He shared with me his strong convictions that the gifts and miraculous power of the Spirit are for today. He spent an afternoon summarizing for me the content of a sermon series he had preached on "The Sealing with the Holy Spirit" and arranged for me to get a copy of a mimeographed set of notes on that series. (The series was later transcribed and published in two volumes by Harold Shaw: *Joy Unspeakable* and *The Sovereign Spirit: Discerning His Gifts*.) Some of what I learned that afternoon can be found in chapter 8 of this book.

In that conversation and one other that same summer, Lloyd-Jones showed a great openness and appreciation for the charismatic renewal and especially the Jesus people movement that was then near its peak. He was convinced that belief in the gifts and miraculous power of the Spirit was not only consistent with what we called "the Reformed Faith" (Calvinism) but was the teaching of the English

Puritans, including those who wrote the Westminster Confession of Faith.

Lloyd-Jones' influence that summer was a major factor in my new openness to the work of the Spirit and in the beginnings of the pilgrimage that has led to the writing of this book.

Ten years ago I was open to the work of the Spirit and seeking to learn more about it. At the same time I was cautious and critical of the charismatic renewal and of many practices I considered unbiblical. I was (and still am) critical of telling people that they would certainly be healed except for their lack of faith; of acting as if tongues-speaking Christians have attained a level of super-spirituality that others lack; of giving "prophecies" that manipulate people or pretend to be messages from God that He failed to put in the Bible but is now giving His more advanced prophets.

In the years since that conversation with Dr. Lloyd-Jones, and especially in the last ten years, I have learned to appropriate the best things from the renewal and integrate them with Reformed theology. I have learned to receive the gifts and power of the Spirit and use them as Jesus intended for the healing of others, and I have learned to make healing ministry a significant part of my work as an evangelist.

I am writing this book for readers who are in a place similar to mine ten years ago. You are active, witnessing Christians, many of you in historic denominations, and are open to the supernatural dimension of the Christian life. You would like to appropriate the gifts and power of the Spirit and use them for healing others. You would like to see your witnessing strengthened by adding the element of healing.

At the same time you have serious reservations because you, too, have been burned by bad experiences with charismatics and see much in the movement that is unbiblical. Like me, you want to incorporate the best from that movement but do it cautiously and integrate what you receive with what you understand to be sound biblical theology.

I am writing for someone who is both open and cautious. You are willing to read an entry-level how-to manual on healing evangelism, but you want that manual to grapple with some of the theological issues that hinder you from full participation in this kind of ministry.

Some readers will be Presbyterians like me for whom the integration of conclusions with my theology will be especially helpful. Most readers, however, will be from a broad cross-section of denominations and will, I hope, benefit from my efforts to integrate spiritual experience with the historic Christian faith. Non-Presbyterians will forgive me, I trust, for my many illustrations about Presbyterians. They are the people I know best. But with a little reflection I am sure you can come up with as many illustrations from your own tradition. In fact, I challenge you to do so.

Because many readers will need more theological perspective than fits conveniently into a how-to-do-it manual, I am adding a few appendixes that are more theological in nature. I hope you will consider them a valuable part of this volume.

In the next chapter I will argue that healing should be part of our evangelism, as it was for Christ and the apostles. It will be followed by three chapters explaining why not everyone is healed. These next four chapters, constituting parts 1 and 2 of this book, lay a theological foundation for healing evangelism and show how to conduct the ministry without giving the impression that, if someone is not healed, it is his or her fault for not having enough faith.

Once this foundation is laid, this book clearly takes on its character as a how-to manual. Part 3 deals with things you need to be effective in healing evangelism: faith, victory in spiritual warfare, power as a result of prayer, the gifts of the Spirit and the guidance of the Spirit. Part 4 offers instructions for three particular aspects of healing evangelism: the use of "action prayers," deliverance from oppression by evil spirits and inner healing. Part 5 provides details for doing healing evangelism in different settings. And in part 6 I try to pull things together to help you get started.

Healing Evangelism for You and Me

You have probably already surmised that this is not a book about Pentecostal evangelism or even about charismatic evangelism. I am not asking you to change your theology except where it might state that healing miracles and gifts of the Spirit, particularly gifts related to healing, are not for today. (More about this in chapter 2.) Nor am I asking you to change your basic evangelistic methods or join any new movement. Nor will this book tell you everything you need to know to do evangelism, since you already know what the Gospel is and how to present it, and many of you are presenting it very well.

I am simply asking one thing of you—that you incorporate healing prayer into your evangelistic methodology. By doing this, you turn your evangelism into healing evangelism. It may or may not become a major emphasis. That is up to you, as you are led by the Spirit.

Please notice that when Jesus spoke of casting out demons and laying hands on the sick and seeing them recover, He was speaking of signs that "will accompany those who believe" (Mark 16:17). These are the privilege of all believers, not just apostles, deeply devoted saints or professional healing evangelists. They belong to the lay people of the Yoido Full Gospel Church and the Glendale Presbyterian Church. And if you are a believer, they belong to you!

But, you might ask, are these signs really for today? Wasn't that teaching only for the apostolic age? Does Jesus really expect us in the twentieth century to do evangelism the way He did it in the first?

These are the questions we will consider in the next chapter.

2

The Evangelism of Jesus Is for Today

In the ministry of Jesus, healing was not a gimmick to draw crowds. Nor was it a benefit He separated from the preaching of His evangelistic message. Healing was integral to His message and expressive of it.

The message involved the Kingdom of God. "The time has come," He said. "The kingdom of God is near. Repent and believe the good news!" (Mark 1:15; see Matthew 4:17). This was the same message preached by John the Baptizer (Matthew 3:2). The Kingdom or reign of God, which since the time of John had been "forcefully advancing" (Matthew 11:12), had come to earth in Christ. John urged people to repent so that they could enter that Kingdom and submit to that reign.

Advancing the Kingdom of God means pushing back the kingdom of Satan, which currently reigns on earth. Jesus said:

> If I drive out demons by the Spirit of God, then the kingdom of God has come upon you. Or again, how can any-

> one enter a strong man's house and carry off his possessions unless he first ties up the strong man? Then he can rob his house.
>
> Matthew 12:28–29

> On this rock I will build my church, and the gates of Hades will not overcome it. I will give you the keys of the kingdom of heaven; whatever you bind on earth will be bound in heaven, and whatever you loose on earth will be loosed in heaven.
>
> Matthew 16:18–19

An important element of pushing back the kingdom of darkness is providing forgiveness and victory over sin. As John wrote, "He who does what is sinful is of the devil, because the devil has been sinning from the beginning. The reason the Son of God appeared was to destroy the devil's work" (1 John 3:8). Sin, misery, disease and death are works of Satan that came into the world with the Fall. They are means by which Satan oppresses those God made in His image. Because God loves us so much, the devil hates us and seeks to keep us in misery and bondage.

As the New Testament unfolds we learn that destroying the devil's work is the most basic part of Christ's work, because it facilitates reconciliation with God. Jesus entered a world in which people were bound by Satan into sin, misery, disease and death, and came to destroy the works of Satan and set people free.

The opportunity for freedom from the oppression of Satan is at the heart of the passage from Isaiah that Jesus read in the synagogue at Nazareth at the beginning of His public ministry:

> The Spirit of the Lord is on me,
> because he has anointed me
> to preach good news to the poor.

He has sent me to proclaim freedom for the prisoners
and recovery of sight for the blind,
to release the oppressed,
to proclaim the year of the Lord's favor.

Luke 4:18–19

When the teachers of the Law questioned Jesus' power to forgive sins, He demonstrated it by healing the paralytic. "Which is easier," he asked them, "to say to the paralytic, 'Your sins are forgiven,' or to say, 'Get up, take your mat and walk'?" (Mark 2:9; see Matthew 9:5; Luke 5:23).

Thus, the work of healing is not separate from the preaching of forgiveness. Healing is a clear demonstration of Jesus' authority to forgive us and make us right with God.

Why Did Jesus Heal?

There were several motives that drove Christ's healings. First, He was demonstrating His power over Satan so that people could receive His message, repent and enter God's Kingdom. Second, He had compassion on people in bondage to the works of Satan. Jesus longed for people to be delivered from Satan's kingdom, through faith and repentance, to become children of God.

Let's look at these motives one at a time.

Authentication

Some say that the sole purpose of the miracles performed by Jesus and the apostles was to demonstrate the truth of the Gospel. The message was new and needed to be verified. Now that the New Testament is written, say these cessationist brothers and sisters, the message is no longer new, there is no longer any need for miracles and they have ceased.

First, let's consider whether the miracles confirmed the message because it was (then) brand-new revelation or because it is the eternal Gospel. After all, this Gospel is new to every generation and person who first hears it. And since deliverance from the works of Satan is an integral part of the message, isn't it reasonable to expect that healings will take place whenever the message is preached, especially when it is preached to a people group for the first time?

The author of Hebrews testifies:

> . . . This salvation, which was first announced by the Lord, was confirmed to us by those who heard him. God also testified to it by signs, wonders and various miracles, and gifts of the Holy Spirit distributed according to his will.
>
> Hebrews 2:3–4

Paul said of his ministry:

> I will not venture to speak of anything except what Christ has accomplished through me in leading the Gentiles to obey God by what I have said and done—by the power of signs and miracles, through the power of the Spirit.
>
> Romans 15:18–19

The message was first proclaimed by Jesus and the disciples with acts of healing and deliverance that confirmed and demonstrated it. So shouldn't healing and deliverance be part of our preaching today?

Compassion

The confirmation of new revelation is not the only purpose of miracles. Jesus healed out of compassion to deliver people in bondage to the works of Satan. Even if we granted that the need for authentication has ceased, the compassion of Jesus continues, along with the need for miracles.

Healing was a concrete expression of the compassion of God for a lost world. When Jesus healed, He was demonstrating God's love in ways that people could understand. And they *did* understand:

> The people were all so amazed that they asked each other, "What is this? A new teaching—and with authority! He even gives orders to evil spirits and they obey him."
>
> Mark 1:27

We will return to the issues raised by those who believe that miracles have ceased and that healing evangelism should not be practiced today. First, however, let's look at the instructions Jesus gave to His evangelistic teams. Some objections to doing healing evangelism today are based on these instructions.

Healing by Jesus' Evangelistic Teams

First Jesus divided the disciples into six two-man teams. Later He sent out 36 two-man teams. Their ministry: preaching, teaching, healing and deliverance. His commissioning of these evangelistic teams is found in Matthew, Mark and Luke:

> As you go, preach this message: "The kingdom of heaven is near." Heal the sick, raise the dead, cleanse those who have leprosy, drive out demons.
>
> Matthew 10:7–8

> They went out and preached that people should repent. They drove out many demons and anointed many sick people with oil and healed them.
>
> Mark 6:12–13

> Heal the sick who are there and tell them, "The kingdom of God is near you."
>
> Luke 10:9

Notice that Christ's commissioning included deliverance:

> When Jesus had called the Twelve together, he gave them power and authority to drive out all demons and to cure diseases, and he sent them out to preach the kingdom of God and to heal the sick.
>
> Luke 9:1–2 (see Matthew 10:1)

When the 72 additional evangelists returned they were very excited: "Lord, even the demons submit to us in your name" (Luke 10:17).

Jesus did not feel that this submission justified so much excitement. The reign of evil spirits, he knew, was being crushed by the advance of the Kingdom of God, and their power compared to His was weak and puny. "Do not rejoice that the spirits submit to you," He told them, "but rejoice that your names are written in heaven" (Luke 10:20).

He also told them, "I saw Satan fall like lightning from heaven" (Luke 10:18). This can be understood to refer to Satan's original departure from heaven or to his final defeat at Christ's return. But neither interpretation fits the context well. I believe Christ was commenting here on the tremendous blow that Satan's kingdom was taking from the ministry of the evangelistic teams.

Jesus went on to say, "I have given you authority to trample on snakes and scorpions and to overcome all the power of the enemy" (Luke 10:19a). The context shows clearly that He was referring not to literal snakes and scorpions but to the evil spirits that the evangelistic teams were casting out. Moreover, Jesus was declaring that He had given them so much authority that they were able "to overcome all the power of the enemy."

It can be frightening to realize that you are involved in combat with Satan himself, even if you are on the winning side. So Jesus added this word of assurance and encouragement: "Nothing will harm you" (Luke 10:19b).

Before we determine whether this authority belongs to evangelists today and whether healing and deliverance should be part of our own witnessing, let's look at the instructions Jesus gave His evangelistic teams. They covered three basic topics:

1. What they were to do—preach, heal and cast out demons.
2. How they were to handle rejection and persecution.
3. How they were to conduct themselves on their journeys.

In the first set of instructions Jesus limited their preaching and healing "to the lost sheep of Israel" (Matthew 10:6). (Paul made the same delineation in Romans 1:16 when he said that the Gospel is "first for the Jew, then for the Gentile.") After His resurrection Jesus would command the disciples to be witnesses in "all nations" (Matthew 28:19), in a particular order: "In Jerusalem, and in all Judea and Samaria, and to the ends of the earth" (Acts 1:8). It was not that the evangelistic teams had a message or ministry of healing and deliverance exclusively for Jews. Ultimately it was for all the world. But Jesus, sending them out at the beginning, told them to start with the Jews.

Jesus' second set of instructions, on handling rejection and persecution, has proven invaluable for rejected and persecuted believers in many nations and at all times.

His third set of instructions emphasized that the evangelistic teams were to depend on the hospitality of those to whom they preached. "Whatever town or village you enter," He said, "search for some worthy person there and stay at his house until you leave" (Matthew 10:11). This "worthy person," perhaps a righteous community leader, would in effect become the sponsor of their evangelization efforts in his city or village. He would provide everything they needed, so they were to take no suitcase (or its first-century equivalent), no extra clothing or money. They were to depend entirely on this sponsor (and ultimately on the Lord, who promises we will lack nothing) so that the Gospel would be supported by those who heard it. "Do not take along any gold or silver or copper in your belts," Jesus said. "Take no bag for the journey, or extra tunic, or sandals or a staff; for the worker is worth his keep" (Matthew 10:9–10).

Once they moved in with their host, Jesus told them, they were to stay with him for the rest of their time in that city or village. "Whenever you enter a house," He said, "stay there until you leave that town" (Mark 6:10). Jesus anticipated the possibility that once they had moved in with a host, someone else might come along and offer them more luxurious accommodations. The first sponsor would certainly be offended to have them reject his hospitality and move out while the crusade was in progress. More important, to have the first part of the crusade sponsored by one person and the last part sponsored by another would bring confusion to the ministry and discredit to the evangelists.

Finally, evangelists are to be people of urgency. "Do not greet anyone on the road," Jesus said (Luke 10:4). In a culture that dictated elaborate Oriental rituals of greeting that friends were to follow when meeting one another, Jesus was advocating not unfriendliness but urgency. Evangelists have no time for such things. We bear a life-and-death message. Christ, not culture, must dictate our use of time.

Healing Evangelism Is for Today

I am convinced that healing and deliverance were features not unique to the evangelism of Jesus. He required them of all the teams He commissioned. Evangelistic teams today, like those Jesus sent out long ago, are not only to preach the Gospel but to heal the sick and cast out demons.

Because we have the biblical mandate to do these things, we also have the power. Not only to the disciples but to us belong Jesus' words "I have given you authority to trample on snakes and scorpions and to overcome all the power of the enemy; nothing will harm you" (Luke 10:19). Of our ministries, too, Jesus should be able to say, "I saw Satan fall like lightning from heaven" (verse 18).

In what we call the Great Commission, Jesus told the disciples to teach all nations "to obey everything I have commanded you" (Matthew 28:20). Since Jesus commanded these very same men to "heal the sick, raise the dead, cleanse those who have leprosy, drive out demons" (Matthew 10:8), doesn't it stand to reason that those acts are among the "everything" that He commanded them to teach the nations? If so, then we should be doing those very things.

It is common for people to argue that the instructions given to the evangelistic teams were special instructions for that time only and are exempt from the "everything" we are to teach all nations. They point out that Jesus also said, "Do not go among the Gentiles or enter any town of the Samaritans" (Matthew 10:5).

But after that time Jesus broadened His instructions and said they should go to "Samaria, and to the ends of the earth" (Acts 1:8). That Jesus later broadened the scope of evangelistic activity does not mean that the nature of the activity—preaching and healing—had changed.

Critics further argue that His instructions included not bringing a bag, extra clothing or money. They argue that those of us who believe healing should be part of evangelism today should travel without suitcases, extra clothing and money. To be consistent, we should travel without credit cards, too.

They fail to note that Jesus specifically retracted that part of His instructions on His last night with the disciples before His crucifixion:

> Then Jesus asked them, "When I sent you without purse, bag or sandals, did you lack anything?"
>
> "Nothing," they answered.
>
> He said to them, "But now if you have a purse, take it, and also a bag; and if you don't have a sword, sell your cloak and buy one."
>
> Luke 22:35–36

The principles of simple lifestyle, traveling light, dependence on the Lord and being supported for Gospel preaching remain valid. The specific prohibitions against bags, extra clothing and money no longer apply.

At or near the time of the Great Commission, Jesus specifically withdrew the two details about where to go and what to bring. Does it not follow that everything He did *not* withdraw is still in effect? If so, then part of what we are to teach all nations is to heal the sick and cast out demons.

Critics respond by pointing to the detail about not greeting people on the road. This, they say, was culturally conditioned and not specifically withdrawn by Christ, which proves that all the instructions given to evangelistic teams were for that time only and are exempt from the "everything" we are to teach the nations.

It is true that Jesus did not withdraw that piece of instruction. It is also true that we are to be persons of urgency who govern our time by the dictates of Christ and not culture. As an evangelist, though I have traveled to many places, I have not yet visited a culture that required the elaborate rituals of greeting that existed in Jesus' day. If I ever am, I would consider the teaching of Jesus still valid and would abstain from those cultural forms.

Can the Dead Be Raised Today?

The critics have one more major argument. They point out that Christ's commandments to the disciples—"Heal the sick, raise the dead, cleanse those who have leprosy, drive out demons" (Matthew 10:8)—include the phrase *raise the dead*.

"Surely we cannot be expected to raise the dead today," they argue. "So the rest of the instructions cannot apply to us either."

But the instances of Christ and the apostles raising the dead were examples of resuscitation, not resurrection. Lazarus and the others died again; they rose not in immortal, heavenly bodies but in mortal, earthly bodies.

These resuscitations, rare in biblical times, are also rare in our time. But they do occur. Please allow me to give two examples.

The day after I preached a weekend missions conference in a Presbyterian church in Louisiana, the pastor's wife was involved in a serious automobile accident (as I learned later). Sandra was the one passenger in the car, seated next to the driver. When the ambulance arrived, the paramedics found her dead and began working on the driver, who still had some vital signs.

Soon a church member arrived on the scene. She laid her hands on Sandra and prayed for her. Within minutes, to the astonishment of the paramedics, Sandra regained consciousness. She was admitted to the hospital with a concussion and multiple severe fractures, and made a remarkably fast recovery.

"Anyone who has faith in me," Jesus said, "will do what I have been doing" (John 14:12).

Here is another example of resuscitation. When a longtime friend of mine, Stewart Pohlman, a Presbyterian minister in Montgomery, New York, suffered a severe stroke in May 1991, the hospital staff worked over him with the belief that he was comatose. Actually, Stew could hear them clearly but was unable to respond in any way.

Then he heard them say, "There are no vital signs. We just lost him."

This was no out-of-body experience. Stew was very much in the body. But at that moment his body was clinically dead.

Lord, he prayed, *if You're going to take me to heaven, take me quickly. But if You have more for me to do on earth, then restore my vital signs immediately.*

At that moment his vital signs returned and he regained consciousness.

Stew is in good health today, almost four years later, with absolutely no physical effects from the stroke.

I have heard of a number of people like the pastor's wife who were pronounced dead and then prayed back to life. Stew is the only person I know who has prayed himself back from the dead. But Jesus said, ". . . He will do even greater things than these, because I am going to the Father" (John 14:12).

Miracles in History and Today

We have seen that healing, including casting out demons and resuscitation, was an essential element of the evangelism of Jesus; that He made it an essential element of the evangelistic teams He sent out; that it was so throughout the apostolic age; and that it was to be taught to all nations. Healing should thus be an essential element of our evangelism today.

The argument that miracles ceased immediately after the close of the apostolic age is a theological, not a true historical, argument. It is based on theological assumptions about the uniqueness of the ministry of the apostles, as well as the assumption that the only purpose of miracles is to authenticate brand-new revelation.

Historically it is false to say that miracles stopped after the apostolic age. I direct you to the book *Christian Initiation and Baptism in the Holy Spirit: Evidence from the First Eight Centuries* by Kilian McDonnell and George T. Montague (The Liturgical Press, 1991). This volume consists largely of documentation from the writings of early Church fathers regarding miracles in the Church in the first eight centuries.

And nowhere does the New Testament hint that the gifts of the Spirit will cease. In fact, 1 Corinthians 13:12 says that gifts of the Spirit will not cease until heaven: "Then we shall see face to face. Now I know in part; then I shall know fully, even as I am fully known." I direct you to the further discussion of this subject that appears in appendix 3, "The Gifts and Guidance of the Spirit in the Reformed Tradition" on pp. 238–46.

No, miracles did not cease, nor were they ever withdrawn. The message Christ preached was not for that age or dispensation only, as some people argue, but is eternal. There have been periods when the faith of Christians was weak and miracles rare. But we must not make periods of decline the norm for all times. Rather, we must recover the faith and power of Christ, of His evangelistic teams, of the apostles and of the early Church.

Did Christ and the apostles heal everyone they prayed for completely and instantly? No. Nor can Christians today just go pray and empty out the hospitals. In the next section we will see some reasons why.

Still, Christ's message and His compassion have not changed (Hebrews 13:8). We are all witnesses for Him and should, with His compassion for the suffering, make healing a part of our own evangelism.

Part 2

Why Isn't Everyone Healed?

It is cruel to say, as some do, "You weren't healed because you don't have enough faith." But if the healing power of Jesus Christ is available today, why *isn't* everyone healed instantly and completely?

In this section we will consider a few reasons.

3

The Kingdom Is Here and Yet Not Yet

I wish I could tell you that every sick person I have prayed for was healed quickly or completely. That would not be true, and I cannot claim to be more effective than Jesus and Paul.

Jesus did not heal every sick person He met. There were many disabled at the Pool of Bethesda but He healed only one (John 5:3, 5–6). Jesus followed the leading of His Father as to which works He was to do (John 5:19). On one occasion He declined to heal a sick person when He was asked, instead letting him die (John 11), although later He raised him from the dead. Apparently the Father showed Him that resuscitation, not healing, was the ministry He was to perform for Lazarus.

Nor were all of Jesus' healings instantaneous:

- The blind man at Bethsaida was first healed partially, later completely (Mark 8:22–26). The time frame was short but not instantaneous.
- The lepers in Luke 17:11–19 were not healed until after they left the presence of Jesus.
- The man in John 9:6–7 was blind when he left Jesus' presence. He was not healed until after he washed.
- Jesus was not as successful in healing the sick as He might have been had He found more faith in Nazareth (Matthew 13:53–58; Mark 6:1–6).

The New Testament records other healings that were not complete or that apparently did not take place at all:

- When Ananias laid hands on him, scales fell from Paul's eyes and he was miraculously healed of the blindness that came from the bright light on the Damascus road (Acts 9:18). Yet that healing was not complete. Later he stood by the high priest, who was in full ecclesiastical regalia, and did not recognize him (Acts 23:5). His eye troubles forced him to stop in Galatia, where he found people who came to love him so much that they would have torn out their own eyes and given them to him (Galatians 4:13–15). His poor eyesight required him to write in large letters when he signed the epistles he dictated to others (Galatians 6:11). Red and sore eyes were probably the reason for his unappealing appearance (2 Corinthians 10:10). Three times he pleaded with the Lord to remove his "thorn in the flesh," but the Lord refused because He had something better for him (2 Corinthians 12:7–9).
- Trophimus, an important member of Paul's team, had to be left at Miletus due to illness (2 Timothy 4:20). We may assume that Paul prayed for his heal-

ing, yet he remained sick and was unable to complete the missionary journey.
- Paul's friend Epaphroditus, present with Paul in Rome, was sick for a long time and nearly died (Philippians 2:26–27). Paul's prayers spared Epaphroditus from death but not from a long illness.
- Paul wrote his young friend Timothy with advice on Timothy's stomach trouble and "frequent illnesses" (1 Timothy 5:23). Surely Paul was concerned enough to pray about these illnesses, yet we never hear that Timothy was healed.

So Where Does the Kingdom of God Fit In?

When Jesus said of us, "They will place their hands on sick people, and they will get well" (Mark 16:18), He did not say that *everyone* would get well or that those who did would be healed instantly.

In the same passage He promised deliverance from potentially fatal accidents (snakebites) and from those who would murder us for the sake of the Gospel (deadly poison). But surely Christians have died in fatal accidents; and Jesus taught that many would be martyred for the faith (Matthew 24:9). He specifically predicted the martyrdom of Peter (John 21:18–19). The promised healings and rescues will happen often enough to commend the Gospel to unbelievers, but they are not promised for every single instance.

The Kingdom of God came with the first coming of Christ, who preached that "the kingdom of heaven is near" (Matthew 4:17). He demonstrated the power of that Kingdom as He advanced it against the kingdom of darkness by healing the sick and casting out demons (Matthew 4:23–25). But the Kingdom of God did not come in its fullness. That awaits the Second Coming of Christ "when he hands over the kingdom to God the Father after he has destroyed all dominion, authority and power. For he must reign until he has put all his enemies under his feet" (1 Corinthians 15:24–25).

So the Kingdom of God is here and, in another sense, not yet. The sick are healed, but not all of them, and not all instantaneously and completely. The *presence* of the Kingdom encourages us to pray for ourselves, that it may be true of us that "the power of the Lord [is] present . . . to heal the sick" (Luke 5:17). The *absence* of the consummated Kingdom keeps us from discouragement when we do not see the powerful results we would like.

What Should We Look For?

What, based on the experience and teaching of Jesus Himself, should we expect and teach with regard to healing evangelism?

First, we should not assume that every prayer will lead to instant success, nor should we teach that everyone will be healed instantly who truly believes. That is to distort the Gospel as well as engage in cruelty. Our methods must authenticate and not alter the evangelistic message.

We *should* expect that God will often bring about remarkable healings and that many will receive an immediate healing touch.

What about those who do not? Francis MacNutt has a wonderful concept, described in his book *The Prayer that Heals*, that he calls "soaking prayer." Just as an injured foot may need to be soaked many times in hot water before it is healed, or cancerous tissue may need to be exposed to many strong doses of radiation therapy before it is destroyed, so a person may need to receive "soaking prayer" for long periods of time before he or she is healed.

We should also expect, then, that many will be healed as we offer patient prayers for healing over a period of time.

What of those who are not healed even then? Can we ever say that "by his wounds we are healed" (Isaiah 53:5) when some people we pray for remain sick?

In the following chapter we will discuss whether healing is one of the built-in benefits of Christ's sacrifice on our behalf.

4

Is Healing in the Atonement?

If the heart of our evangelistic message is "Jesus Christ and him crucified" (1 Corinthians 2:2), what is the relationship between the cross of Jesus Christ and physical healing? We have already seen that as we preach the cross, we can pray for the sick and expect to see them healed. But does healing express something that is peripheral to the atonement—Jesus' payment for our sins that put us "at one" with God—or integral to it?

We often hear these days that among the consequences of sin are disease and death, and that Christ died not only for the forgiveness of our sins but for the healing of our diseases. We hear quoted Isaiah 53, a passage that predicts in detail the suffering, death and resurrection of the Messiah, specifically verses 4–5:

> Surely he took up our infirmities
> and carried our sorrows,
> yet we considered him stricken by God,
> smitten by him, and afflicted.

> But he was pierced for our transgressions,
> he was crushed for our iniquities;
> the punishment that brought us peace was upon him,
> and by his wounds we are healed.

Those who teach that the atonement covered our sicknesses, too, stress in particular the last phrase of the above passage: "By his wounds [*stripes* in the KJV] we are healed." They remind us that Isaiah 53:4–5 can be translated, "He has borne our *sicknesses* and carried our *pains*" (RSV footnote, italics added). And they like to point out that Isaiah 53 is interpreted in Matthew 8:16–17, which says:

> When evening came, many who were demon-possessed were brought to him, and he drove out the spirits with a word and healed all the sick. This was to fulfill what was spoken through the prophet Isaiah:
> "He took up our infirmities
> and carried our diseases."

So what about it? *Is* healing part of the atonement?

The Way It Is Preached

Healing as part of the atonement is a theory that disturbs many people, perhaps because of the way it is often preached.

Some say, "When you called on Christ for forgiveness, you were instantly forgiven by the power of His cross. Now call on Him for physical healing. That, too, is in the atonement. As soon as you pray in faith for healing, you will be healed."

Others say, "Because healing is in the atonement, perfect health is your right as a child of God. Just claim it by faith and it will be yours."

Still others argue like this: "Notice that 'By his wounds we are healed' is in the present tense. It may not appear that way to you, since you can see your symptoms of sickness, but you are *already* healed, present tense! You were healed two thousand years ago when Christ paid for your healing on the cross. So the pain you feel or the symptoms of illness you manifest are only illusions sent by the devil to keep you from recognizing the truth that you are already healed. Refuse to accept these illusions and live in the faith that you are healed now."

However these teachings are framed, their conclusion is this: that if you do not enjoy perfect health, there must be something wrong with your faith. Since Christ bought your healing and you are healed already—by his wounds you *are* (not *will be*) healed—you must be refusing to accept it by faith.

Since this is the way "healing is in the atonement" is often preached, it is understandable that many are uncomfortable with it.

My own discomfort with this teaching was intensified by a situation that had the potential to disillusion me, the congregation I was pastoring and many other Christians in the city. Let me tell you what happened.

Joy Anne

In 1976 my wife, Eileen, had a miracle pregnancy. Her tubes had closed after the birth of our son, David, and the doctor said it would be impossible for her to conceive again. But one tube reopened and she did conceive. Then the doctor said it would be impossible for her to carry the child because her womb was inverted, but her womb partly reinverted. Then the doctor said it might be possible for Eileen to carry the baby full-term, but that it was unlikely.

We saw every day as a fresh, new miracle from the Lord.

Joy Anne was born full-term, but hours after her birth the doctors discovered a congenital defect, a diaphragmatic hernia. In those days the odds of a newborn's surviving this were only one in ten.

Our church and many other congregations in the city began to pray for her healing. Eileen and I were gratified there was so much prayer. At the same time I was uncomfortable about the prayers from one church. Believing that healing is in the atonement, they were "claiming" Joy Anne's healing and thanking God in advance for it. This way of praying seemed presumptuous to me. I was not convinced that her healing was guaranteed by the Scriptures nor that we had a right to claim it from God as if it were.

Nevertheless, as surgery was performed, we fully expected her to be healed. God had worked so many miracles to get her here, surely He would work one more to keep her here.

But the Lord took Joy Anne to heaven when she was just a half-hour short of one week old. This was a great blow to many who had prayed in faith. One member of our congregation told me recently that her prayer life was disturbed for years because she was so angry at God that Joy Anne had died when virtually the whole city of Pensacola was praying for her healing.

Eileen and I were established enough in our understanding of God's sovereignty that her death did not shake our faith or disturb our prayer lives. In fact, soon after Joy Anne's death Eileen was comforting herself by reading Ephesians 1, where she discovered that the phrase translated in the King James Version as *the good pleasure of [God's] will* (verse 5) was rendered in her New American Standard Bible as *the kind intention of His will.*

But the people who had "claimed" Joy Anne's healing because it was "in the atonement" let Eileen know that they thought Joy Anne's death was her fault. They said Joy Anne would have lived if only Eileen had had more faith.

Because of the loss of Joy Anne, and because we believed we would never be able to have another child, we experienced a good deal of grief during this period, intensified by the cruelty of those who blamed Eileen for Joy Anne's death. We suffered more because of their faulty theology.

On my first Sunday back in the pulpit, I preached a sermon to reassure the congregation (and Eileen and me) that God had not failed to keep His promises. My text was Ephesians 1:5, and the sermon title, "His Kind Intention." Healing *is* in the atonement, I told them, but heaven is in the atonement, too. When we believe in the Lord Jesus Christ, we are instantly forgiven but we do not instantly go to heaven. Some of the blessings of the atonement we have in a partial sense now, and some we will have in a complete sense in the future, when we get to heaven. One day we shall all be perfectly healed of our diseases when we stand before the throne of the Lamb and sing His praises. It is God's will ultimately that all His people be healed. Sometimes it is His will that we be healed instantly, but sometimes He has something better for us, because our illnesses and infirmities can be part of His wonderful work for our sanctification.

God did not heal Joy Anne in the way we were praying for, I said. He healed her by taking her to heaven.

The sermon seemed to comfort the congregation (I know it comforted me), although some continued to struggle with anger and doubt. The sermon was later printed in several magazines (retitled "The Sovereignty of God in the Death of Our Daughter") and distributed widely as a brochure. Eileen now feels that the principal purpose of Joy Anne's brief life and death was for a sermon to be preached that has brought comfort to many. (How wonderful it is when God reveals to us something of His sovereign purposes for good in what first appears to be tragic!)

The faulty theology of those who "claimed" Joy Anne's healing on the basis of the atonement added not only to our grief but to the doubt, confusion and anger of others. I hope the distribution of my sermon has enabled some to see more clearly what God has actually promised and has prevented some others from suffering the ill consequences of wrong teaching with regard to healing. (More on this erroneous doctrine in appendix 1, "Should Positive Confession Replace Prayer?" on p. 217.)

A year after this experience, incidentally, the Lord enabled Eileen and me to adopt Katy, who was then a year old. The two girls were born only a few months apart. Eileen says, "I have two little girls. One is growing up at home and one is growing up in heaven."

Healing and the Message of the Cross

As we evangelize, we declare that through the cross of Jesus Christ all who believe are made right with God. He no longer counts our sins against us but credits them to Christ, who paid for them with His blood. Credited to our account instead is the perfect, active righteousness of Jesus Christ (2 Corinthians 5:21).

So what can we conclude about healing and the atonement? Recall the passage I quoted at the beginning of this chapter:

> When evening came, many who were demon-possessed were brought to him, and he drove out the spirits with a word and healed all the sick. This was to fulfill what was spoken through the prophet Isaiah:
> "He took up our infirmities
> and carried our diseases."
>
> Matthew 8:16–17

Matthew was telling us that when Jesus healed the sick, He was setting them free from illness in direct fulfillment of Isaiah 53. That beloved Old Testament prophecy cannot be spiritualized to mean that Jesus would take on Himself only our spiritual problems. Matthew saw it fulfilled in the healing of physical illness. And when Isaiah said, "By his wounds we are healed," physical healing was very much a part of what he had in mind.

Christ died to deliver us from sin and *all* its consequences, including disease and death. He died to provide holiness for us in this life and resurrection and glory in the life to come. He did not, in His earthly ministry, tell people to wait for heaven before they could be healed. He healed many of them right then. And He continues to heal many today, though He heals some (like Joy Anne) by taking them to heaven.

When we do healing evangelism—when we pray for the sick and some are healed—we demonstrate the truth of the Gospel. It is a mistake (as we saw in the last chapter) to promise immediate healing for everyone and so give both false hope and false guilt (for not having enough faith). But it is never a mistake to pray for the sick, because we give Jesus an opportunity to heal some immediately in answer to prayer, and to give all believers the hope that they will be healed according to God's will and in His time.

In the next chapter let's consider more of what it means to pray for healing "according to God's will and in His time."

5

Could Job Have Been Healed in a Crusade?

Those who engage in healing evangelism are confronted constantly with mysteries regarding human suffering. Why do certain people suffer and others do not? Why are some persons healed and others are not?

Job, one of the longest books in the Bible, deals entirely with the mystery of suffering. Lengthy conversations are held over why Job is suffering so much. Yet only the reader of the book, and not Job or his friends, is told the main reason for his suffering. God allowed Satan to smite Job so He could demonstrate Job's faithfulness. Even though Satan "afflicted Job with painful sores from the soles of his feet to the top of his head" (2:7), God knew that, contrary to Satan's assertions, Job would not curse God for his suffering.

At the end of the book, when God gets the last word, He says nothing about this demonstration to Satan. He simply asserts His sovereignty—His right to do as He chooses—and insists that Job does not have a right to question His ways:

> Who is this that darkens my counsel
> with words without knowledge?
> Brace yourself like a man;
> I will question you,
> and you shall answer me.
>
> Where were you when I laid the earth's foundation?
> Tell me, if you understand.
> Who marked off its dimensions? Surely you know!
> Who stretched a measuring line across it?
> On what were its footings set,
> or who laid its cornerstone—
> while the morning stars sang together
> and all the angels shouted for joy?
>
> Job 38:2–7

God had a perfectly good reason for allowing Satan to smite Job. We, the readers, know this. But Job does not need to know the reason. He needs to know only that God has purposes that human beings may never understand. More important than Job's knowing the reason for his suffering is his knowing that God is God, that He has His own reasons and that He has the right to do as He wishes, according to His plan.

Job responds to God by saying:

> I know that you can do all things;
> no plan of yours can be thwarted.
> You asked, "Who is this that obscures my counsel without knowledge?"
> Surely I spoke of things I did not understand,
> things too wonderful for me to know.

> You said, "Listen now, and I will speak;
> I will question you,
> and you shall answer me."
> My ears had heard of you
> but now my eyes have seen you.
> Therefore I despise myself
> and repent in dust and ashes.
>
> Job 42:2–6

Mysteries of God's Will

There are many mysteries about God's will.

We know, for example, that God loves righteousness and hates sin. He wants everyone to keep His holy Law. Yet He has not created a sinless world. The presence of evil is a mystery even more profound than the existence of suffering.

Here is another mystery. We know that God has sent His Son as a sacrifice for the sins of the world. We know that God wants people to come to Jesus for salvation, and that when they come it is because He has drawn them (John 6:37, 44). God also "wants all men to be saved and to come to a knowledge of the truth" (1 Timothy 2:4). Yet God does not draw all to Christ. Instead He says, "I will have mercy on whom I have mercy, and I will have compassion on whom I have compassion" (Romans 9:15; see Exodus 33:19). And, in seeming contrast to this clear assertion of God's sovereignty, Jesus exclaimed over Jerusalem, "How often I have longed to gather your children together, as a hen gathers her chicks under her wings, but you were not willing!" (Luke 13:34).

How can these things be reconciled? We do not know, nor is it for us to know. We are to believe in the goodness of God and acknowledge that He is for righteousness and salvation, even when He does things that seem inconsistent to us.

We have many questions about the mysteries of God's sovereign will. Perhaps the best answer is the one Moses gave:

> The secret things belong to the LORD our God, but the things revealed belong to us and to our children forever, that we may follow all the words of this law.
>
> Deuteronomy 29:29

God has revealed many things to us, but there are secret things He has chosen not to reveal. The answers to our questions about why evil exists, why all are not brought to Christ, why some (including some very righteous persons) suffer and others do not, why some we pray for are healed and others (whom we may pray for more earnestly) are not—all these are included in the realm of the secret things.

Mysteries About Healing

The disciples of Jesus were puzzled over the cause of a man's blindness. They held the same view as Job's tormentors—that anyone who suffers is being punished for a particular sin. But this man was blind at birth. How could he be being punished if he was blind before he could sin? Was he being punished for his parents' sin?

Jesus rejected the notion of suffering as necessarily being punishment for particular sins:

> "Neither this man nor his parents sinned," said Jesus, "but this happened so that the work of God might be displayed in his life."
>
> John 9:3

And then Jesus healed the blind man, thus displaying the work of God in his life.

We have many questions that God will not answer, at least not in this life. It is not wrong to ask questions, but it *is* wrong to demand answers from God or to question Him in the sense of accusing Him of wrongdoing.

We know that God is good, so we must learn to lay our questions aside and worship Him. If we could understand all God's ways, we would be as intelligent as He is. If God were obligated to answer all our questions, *we* ourselves would be God. No, God has purposely kept many things secret from us so that we can sing:

> Oh, the depth of the riches of the wisdom and knowledge of God!
>   How unsearchable his judgments,
>   and his paths beyond tracing out!
> "Who has known the mind of the Lord?
>   Or who has been his counselor?"
> "Who has ever given to God,
>   that God should repay him?"
> For from him and through him and to him are all things.
>   To him be the glory forever! Amen.
>
> Romans 11:33–36

Is Sickness Ever God's Will?

When a child is sick, the mother may administer medicine or call the doctor. She gives little thought to it; it is what she must do. A Christian mother will also pray for her child's healing—but she may tack onto her prayer the phrase *If it be Thy will*. Is this mother "obligated" as a Christian submitted to the will of the Father to pray this way?

Some people believe that sickness is a cross we are to bear, and they cite Jesus' words as proof: "If anyone would come after me, he must deny himself and take up his cross daily and follow me" (Luke 9:23). But Christ took up the suffering of the cross voluntarily for our sake, and He means for us also to suffer voluntarily for His sake—to go to a difficult mission field or be persecuted by unbelievers for the sake of the Gospel or endure some other hardship. The cross Jesus commanded us to bear is not having a cold, not even having cancer.

So can that mother ask God unequivocally for her child's healing, or must she add the clause *If it be Thy will*?

We are guilty of a strange inconsistency when we tack this qualifying phrase onto our prayers for healing. We see nothing wrong with taking medicine or calling the doctor but something very wrong with praying for healing without praying, "If it be Thy will." At the very least, perhaps, we are uncomfortable theologically unless we pray this way. But if a sickness is God's will and we are going against His will by praying an unqualified prayer for healing (one without *If it be Thy will*), then are we not also going against God's will by taking some pills or calling the doctor?

Sickness is no more God's will than sin and unbelief are His will. God is always on the side of healing, just as He is always on the side of righteousness and faith. And ultimate healing for His people is always God's will. But there are mysteries about God's plan. We know He allows and uses things of which He does not approve, and His plan for human history includes sin, unbelief, sickness, even death. God used Joseph's slavery in Egypt to deliver many people, though He did not approve of Joseph's being sold as a slave (Genesis 45:7–8; 50:20). God used the murder of Christ as the center of His plan of redemption, although that murder was wickedness (Acts 2:23).

The mystery here is that God does not approve of sickness any more than He approves of slavery and murder. But that does not mean He always heals. In fact, sometimes He actually uses sickness for our sanctification.

So instead of praying, "If it be Thy will," we should pray for healing "according to Your will." Healing *is* His will; it's just that His timing is not always immediate.

So What About that Healing Crusade?

Here, then, is the big question: What if Job had lived in our century and a healing evangelist had laid hands on him and anointed him with oil? Would Job have been healed?

I believe the answer is yes—but only if God had accomplished four things in Job's life:

1. If God had proved to Satan that Job was faithful and would not curse Him;
2. If He had rebuked the false theories of Job's tormentors;
3. If He had taught Job and others about His sovereignty;
4. If He had taught Job about forgiveness and prayer.

Let's look at these accomplishments one by one.

First, God did disprove Satan's challenge after allowing him to afflict His servant Job.

Second, regarding the false theories of Job's tormentors, God told them, "You have not spoken of me what is right, as my servant Job has" (42:7). Job was not being punished for sin, as they insisted.

Third, as for Job's learning about God's sovereignty, listen again to Job's words:

> My ears had heard of you
>   but now my eyes have seen you.
> Therefore I despise myself
>   and repent in dust and ashes.
>
> Job 42:5–6

And fourth, after telling Job's tormentors to offer sacrifices, God said, "My servant Job will pray for you, and I will accept his prayer and not deal with you according to your folly" (42:8). It could not have been easy for Job to pray for forgiveness for men who had abused him so badly. But he did so, and we are told that it was "after Job had prayed for his friends [that] the LORD made him prosperous again and gave him twice as much as he had before" (42:10). Is it possible that God is withholding blessings from some of us because He is waiting for us to pray for forgiveness for those who have mistreated us?

God finally healed Job, prospered him and restored to him double everything he had lost (42:10) because God had accomplished these four things, and Job was ready for healing.

Let's turn the question around: What if a healing evangelist had laid hands on Job before these four things had been accomplished? Would he have been healed then? The answer is no. Similarly, I believe that many are not healed by our prayers not because they lack faith or because we have failed, but because it is not yet God's time. Nor does God have to tell us His reasons. On the other hand, the more we pray for the sick, the more we will find that it is God's time to heal many.

In the coming section we will investigate some of the elements (faith is the first one) that we need to be effective in healing evangelism.

Part 3

What You Need to Do Healing Evangelism

Although I recommend the ministry of healing evangelism for every believer, not every believer will be equally effective. What makes the difference?

In this section we will look at some of the elements a ministry of healing evangelism needs in order to be effective: faith, victory in spiritual warfare, power in prayer, the gifts of the Holy Spirit and His guidance.

6

All Things Are Possible

One evening the Lord gave me a special turning point in my experience of faith and prayer.

It came while I was pastor of McIlwain Presbyterian Church in Pensacola, Florida. A family that visited our church occasionally requested a visit. Mrs. Scott had just been diagnosed with terminal cancer and given six months to live. She wanted me to come and pray for her.

Until then, when I prayed for the sick, I usually prayed one of those timid, "if-it-be-Thy-will" prayers that we discussed in the last chapter—prayers people expect from Presbyterian ministers. But that evening when I went over to their home, I was led by the Spirit to pray with unusual boldness, earnestness and faith. I had never prayed in just that way before, but I felt constrained by the Lord.

Only years later did I learn what happened. Mrs. Scott awoke the next morning feeling great. She went to the doctor, was examined and told, after tests, that every trace of the cancer was gone. That was more than fifteen years ago.

She is still in good health today and credits her healing to my prayer.

I am enormously grateful that the Lord gave me special faith and earnestness that evening. I did not pray again in that way for several years. But when I learned of the woman's recovery, it strengthened my faith to pray more boldly and earnestly for the healing of others.

The Role of Faith in Healing

The New Testament often points up the important role that faith plays in healings and other miracles—faith in the person being prayed for; in friends, family and community; and in the person doing the praying. Listen to these words of Jesus (duplicate passages included for shades of variation):

> I tell you the truth, if you have faith as small as a mustard seed, you can say to this mountain, "Move from here to there" and it will move. Nothing will be impossible for you.
>
> Matthew 17:20–21

> I tell you the truth, if you have faith and do not doubt, not only can you do what was done to the fig tree, but also you can say to this mountain, "Go, throw yourself into the sea," and it will be done. If you believe, you will receive whatever you ask for in prayer.
>
> Matthew 21:21–22

> Everything is possible for him who believes.
>
> Mark 9:23

> I tell you the truth, if anyone says to this mountain, "Go, throw yourself into the sea," and does not doubt in his heart but believes that what he says will happen, it will be done

> for him. Therefore I tell you, whatever you ask for in prayer, believe that you have received it, and it will be yours.
>
> Mark 11:23–24

> If you have faith as small as a mustard seed, you can say to this mulberry tree, "Be uprooted and planted in the sea," and it will obey you.
>
> Luke 17:6

> [Peter,] beginning to sink, cried out, "Lord, save me!" Immediately Jesus reached out his hand and caught him. "You of little faith," he said, "why did you doubt?"
>
> Matthew 14:30–31

These Scriptures apply directly to us who seek to see diseases uprooted and thrown into the sea. To be used by the Lord for wonderful things in healing evangelism, we need faith and prayer.

The Faith of the Sick Person

Other Scripture passages speak of the faith of the person being healed:

> Jesus turned and saw her. "Take heart, daughter," he said, "your faith has healed you." And the woman was healed from that moment.
>
> Matthew 9:22

> He said to her, "Daughter, your faith has healed you. Go in peace and be freed from your suffering."
>
> Mark 5:34

> "Go," said Jesus, "your faith has healed you." Immediately he received his sight and followed Jesus along the road.
>
> Mark 10:52

> Paul looked directly at him, saw that he had faith to be healed and called out, "Stand up on your feet!" At that, the man jumped up and began to walk.
>
> Acts 14:9–10

The Faith of Family and Community

Still other Scriptures speak of the role played in healing by the faith of friends, family and community:

> Then Jesus answered, "Woman, you have great faith! Your request is granted." And her daughter was healed from that very hour.
>
> Matthew 15:28

> Then Jesus said to the centurion, "Go! It will be done just as you believed it would." And his servant was healed at that very hour.
>
> Matthew 8:13 (see Luke 7:9–10)

> When Jesus saw their faith, he said to the paralytic, "Son, your sins are forgiven. . . . I tell you, get up, take your mat and go home."
>
> Mark 2:5, 11

We find no indication in the three Scripture passages above of faith on the part of the girl, the servant or the paralytic. Rather, the passages suggest that faith was present in the persons who brought them to be healed: in the account of the girl, her mother; with the servant, his centurion master; and with the paralytic, the friends who brought him to Jesus.

Nor is Jairus, the synagogue ruler, commended for his faith, although he was certainly manifesting some by bringing Jesus to raise his dead daughter. "Don't be afraid;

just believe," Jesus told him (Mark 5:36). Jairus' faith, though weak, had to be a contributing factor to the raising of his daughter.

It is significant that when Jesus went to her room to raise her, He dismissed the mourners, who had begun to scoff, but allowed Jairus and his wife to stay, along with the disciples. Frequently in the Bible, when someone intends to resuscitate a dead person, he first asks everyone or almost everyone to leave. This suggests to me that the faith or unbelief of others (and who can condemn anyone for not believing that the dead will be raised?) will hinder the power needed to bring the person back from the dead.

In addition to the dismissal of the scoffers before the resuscitation of Jairus' daughter, note the following:

> "Give me your son," Elijah replied. He took him from her arms, carried him to the upper room where he was staying, and laid him on his bed.
>
> 1 Kings 17:19

> When Elisha reached the house, there was the boy lying dead on his couch. He went in, shut the door on the two of them and prayed to the LORD.
>
> 2 Kings 4:32–33

> Peter sent them all out of the room; then he got down on his knees and prayed. Turning toward the dead woman, he said, "Tabitha, get up." She opened her eyes, and seeing Peter she sat up.
>
> Acts 9:40

Perhaps for a similar reason, Jesus took a deaf man away from the crowd to heal him (Mark 7:33) and led a blind man outside the village, away from the people who brought him, in order to heal him (Mark 8:23).

A further indication that the faith or unbelief of others affects healings is seen in the fact that the miracle-working capability of Jesus was limited by the lack of faith of the people in Nazareth: "He could not do any miracles there, except lay his hands on a few sick people and heal them. And he was amazed at their lack of faith" (Mark 6:5–6).

The Faith of the Person Praying

The faith of the person praying is a major factor in healing. So it is good (as we saw in the last section) to conduct healing evangelism in situations where those present will aid the process by their faith rather than hinder it by unbelief.

While the faith of the person being prayed for can also be a factor, one should never say, "You weren't healed because you didn't have enough faith." You do not know why, in the sovereignty of God, that person was not healed on that day. Even if lack of faith was a factor, it was more likely *your* lack of faith. It is the evangelist who is to have the faith to move mountains.

If someone says to you, "I don't have enough faith to be healed," you can reply, "Perhaps I have enough faith. Rely on mine."

You can also point out that it is not the quantity but the object of the faith that is most important. The woman with the issue of blood did not need to run up to Jesus and hug Him. She touched only the hem of His garment to be healed (Mark 5:25–29). Just a little touch of faith puts us in contact with God's almighty power. Jesus compared faith not to the mountain that was cast into the sea but to the mustard seed.

Levels of Faith in Healing Evangelism

As we practice healing evangelism, we can utilize five types or levels of faith.

The first of these is *saving faith.* This is the most basic kind of faith. It is what has united us to Christ and keeps us in Christ. It is a gift of God. Saving faith is in us because of the supernatural activity of the Holy Spirit and will never leave us. Many Scriptures indicate that saving faith and the repentance that accompanies it are gifts of God and that we come to Christ only because the Lord draws us to Himself. Among these Scriptures are John 6:37, 44; Acts 11:18; 13:48; 16:14; Romans 8:28–30; Ephesians 1:4–5; 2:4–5, 8–9; 2 Thessalonians 2:13–14; 2 Timothy 2:25 and 1 Peter 1:2. This saving faith is the foundation on which all other faith grows.

The second level of faith is *faith that Christ is present with healing power* (Luke 5:17; 6:19). This faith, like every other true faith, is a gift of God to us. Sometimes in doing healing evangelism, we feel the powerful presence of the Lord and see it manifest in particular ways. At other times we may have little sense of the presence of the Lord but believe Jesus is here because we have prayed for His power and Christ will be faithful to answer prayer.

The third level of faith that we can utilize is *faith that Jesus is able to do what we ask.* We are not certain that He *will* do what we are asking Him—heal the sick person or drive out demons—but we know that He *can*. This faith rests on our awareness of Christ's almighty power. It is faith in who He is and what He is able to do. In one sense this faith is more basic than faith that He is present in power on a particular occasion. In another sense it is easier to believe in Christ's presence than to believe He is actually capable of healing the needy person you are ministering to.

The fourth level is *faith that Jesus will do special things*. When I hold a crusade service, many people usually come forward for prayer. Some of them are obviously severely ill or injured. I cannot say for sure that any one of them in particular will be healed, but I am aware that the Lord will heal a number of them. I have faith that at the conclusion of the service many will testify of healing. Exactly what Jesus will do and whom He will heal, I cannot say, but I know He is going to do special things.

The final level of faith we can utilize in healing evangelism is *faith that Jesus will do a particular thing*. This is the faith that Jesus spoke of in the verses we looked at at the beginning of this chapter. We may know that the mountain or mulberry tree will rise up and cast itself into the sea. How is this faith attained? Only as the Lord shows us specifically what He intends to bring to pass. On a certain occasion I may know for sure that a certain person will be healed. Once we receive this insight, we need only express faith in what the Lord has shown us for it to happen.

How Faith Grows

Many Christians rarely have faith beyond the first level. One reason is that faith comes to us only as we need it. Just as in the physical realm we grow by exercise and we atrophy if we do not, so, too, faith needs exercise to grow. Only as we step out in seeking to heal the sick or be used by the Lord in other special ways will we need and receive faith of a higher level. But as we seek to do more for God, we will rise to higher levels of faith.

When I started out in my evangelistic ministry, healing was not part of it. But as I traveled to developing countries, people came to me after services and asked me to pray for their healing. I felt awkward, but I did so. Imagine my surprise when some told me they felt better immediately and were sure my prayer had contributed to their healing!

It was hard to believe at first, but as time went on I grew in confidence that the Lord was using my prayers for the sick. In time not only did I pray when people asked me, but I took the initiative in offering to pray. Later I began praying for the sick, not just privately after services but publicly during those services. Even later, prayer for the sick became a regular part of my evangelistic missions.

A major factor in this growth was my work with indigenous evangelists who had healing ministries and who I knew were genuine. I learned much from ministering with them and observing their healing evangelism. Much of my faith was caught and learned from them.

Your faith will grow, too, as you move out in the power of the Spirit to do healing evangelism. At the same time, of course, your faith will be under attack. The more you move in the power of the Spirit, the more you will be opposed by demonic spirits. So in addition to faith, you need victory in spiritual warfare—another of the elements of effective healing evangelism. We will examine this element in the next chapter.

7

Not Against Flesh and Blood

Everyone doing healing evangelism is engaged in spiritual warfare. It is by the power of the kingdom of Satan, after all, that people are afflicted with sin, disease and demons. And as the Kingdom of God advances, the kingdom of darkness is pushed back and people are set free. So in order to understand healing prayer, we need to understand spiritual warfare and the role of prayer in that warfare.

Recall C. S. Lewis' theory in *The Screwtape Letters* that Satan has two opposite strategies, and let me identify these strategies by way of my experiences as an evangelist in Uganda. In countries like the U.S. (this is the first strategy) Satan hides himself and cons us into believing he does not exist. But in countries like Uganda (this is the second strategy) he comes out into the open to terrify people into submission.

Things happen in Uganda that are difficult for Americans to conceive. Everywhere are mud-brick, thatch-roofed buildings used as shrines for the worship of the spirits. In the center of these shrines a fire of hot coals is often kept burning. During services it is common for the witch doctor or high priestess to sit in the coals, by the power of the spirits, without being burned. This is no trick or illusion. My friend Enfrance, who was a witch doctor before being led to Christ by Peterson Sozi some years ago, has told me of sitting in the fire and eating the coals by the power of demons.

Patrick Kigozi, one of Uganda's most powerful witch doctors until he was converted through Peterson's Back to God Evangelistic Association in 1990, told me of his training in witchcraft. To prove he was really controlled by spirits, he had to lick a red-hot iron with his tongue, quench a flaming fire with his body and survive outdoors in the jungle among the wild animals for weeks at a time.

But Western missionaries who came to Uganda one hundred years ago told prospective converts, "You people are too superstitious! You're all afraid of evil spirits. There *are* no evil spirits."

This is like going to America and saying there is no such thing as electricity. The power is evident everywhere.

"The white man just doesn't understand," the Ugandans reasoned.

So they joined the white man's church for its financial, medical, social and educational benefits. (Almost eighty percent of Ugandans today are baptized Roman Catholics and Anglicans. Enfrance was an active Anglican the whole time she was a witch doctor.) But because the spirits that the white man does not believe in still need to be appeased, the people wear talismans under their clothing to ward them off. On Sundays they go to church but during the week they worship at the shrines and visit the witch doctor. They know the witch doctor can heal (although not every time) by the power of Satan. The same spirits that afflict us with disease can remove the disease when it suits their purposes.

But a new message is being preached in Uganda and across sub-Saharan Africa—a message through which thousands every day are becoming Christians. The message as delivered by the Ugandans themselves goes something like this:

> The missionaries told us that the little gods [*lubaale*] we worship aren't real. But I tell you they are real and powerful. The supreme Creator-God [*Katonda* in Luganda] has a name for them. He calls them "unclean spirits." They are filthy and defile everyone who worships them. One day Katonda will take these little gods and cast them all into hell. And everyone who has been defiled by them must go into hell with them.
>
> But Katonda doesn't want to send you to hell. That is why He has sent His Son, Jesus, into the world. The *lubaale* are real and powerful, but Jesus is more real and more powerful. He can set you free from these spirits that have kept you and your ancestors in bondage and fear for centuries.
>
> In order to know the deliverance and protection of Jesus, you must become a Christian—not in the white man's sense but in the Bible's sense.
>
> You may have learned from the missionary that the way to become a Christian is to be baptized with a Western name. (Any African name is a pagan name; any Western name is a Christian name.) But I tell you that to become a Christian you must repent of all your witchcraft, renounce all the *lubaale* you have worshiped, take everything you have used for witchcraft and bring it to the preacher for burning.
>
> Don't be afraid of burning these things. The *lubaale* would like to retaliate and harm you, but if you rely on the protection of Jesus they cannot.

When this message is preached, Jesus demonstrates His power by casting out demons, healing the sick and winning power encounters against the *lubaale*. People are thus encouraged to turn from the little gods that hate them to the true God who loves them and to His Son, Jesus Christ.

Those who become Christians continue to believe in the existence of spirits but they no longer fear them. Syncretism ends as they burn their fetishes (items used for witchcraft) and are set free by Jesus. They no longer visit the witch doctor. They have seen that Jesus has the greater power and do not hesitate to pray to Him for healing.

These people have always known the importance of prayer. It was by prayer and ritual that for centuries they sought to appease the *lubaale*. Now they know it is by prayer through Jesus' name that they triumph over the evil spirits.

The typical prayer meeting in a Ugandan church starts on Friday night and lasts until sunrise on Saturday morning. And no wonder! If we understood what they understand, we would pray that intensely, too. Persons with animistic worldviews are not often won to Christ by arguments but by demonstrations of His power in healing evangelism—an essential method of evangelism for missionaries in these cultures.

Nor is the U.S. immune to the presence of evil spirits, as Peterson Sozi found on one of his first trips to this country.

He was standing in a crowd in Woolworth's in downtown Philadelphia on a big sale day. People were jostling against one another, pushing to get waited on. Then a woman next to him happened to glance at him. A look of surprised recognition on her face changed abruptly to the glaring hate stare of a demonized person. Then she let out a horrible scream and pushed her way past shocked customers out of the store.

It seems apparent that a spirit in her had recognized him. Perhaps it was a spirit he had cast out some time before in Uganda that, thousands of miles away, had looked up, seen a familiar face and realized it needed to get out of the store as fast as possible!

At the present time many spirits are being cast out in Africa, China and Latin America. Many of them, "[going] through arid places seeking rest" (Luke 11:24), may be coming to the U.S., which could help explain the rapid rise here of neopaganism and the New Age movement.

Headquarters of the *Lubaale*

A certain hill near the traditional tombs of the royal family, just a short walk from Peterson's home, was a center of witchcraft. Many sacrifices were offered there, including human. Some years ago the hill was sold and the new owner, a man we'll call Mukasa, built a house on the hill. There was no problem building there; the spirits were happy to have a house to live in. But when people came to furnish the house, problems began. When they left the house to walk down the hill, for example, they would hear noises. Looking back, they would see mattresses flying out of the windows of the empty structure. And everyone who spent a night there was dead the next morning.

After several attempts at occupancy, the house sat vacant for a long time.

One day just a few years ago, a Pentecostal bishop I know approached the owner of the hill.

"What are you going to do with the hill and the house?" he asked.

"I don't know," Mukasa said. "It's useless. I can't rent it and I'm certainly not going to stay there myself."

"Our church can use the house and the hill," said the bishop. "We can command the spirits to leave in the name of Jesus."

"If you can spend a night in the house and be alive the next morning, the house and the hill belong to you and the church."

The bishop and his adherents from the World Evangelical Church held an all-night prayer meeting in the house. In the morning they were alive and the spirits were gone. Soon a Christian community connected to the World Evangelical Church lived in the house and farmed the hillside. A church was built behind the house. And the name of the hill was changed to Zion Prayer Mountain.

Because people in developing nations, like those at Zion Prayer Mountain, recognize the reality of spirits in our present world, their worldview is closer to the biblical worldview than that of modern secular humanists. Only as we in the West begin to take more seriously the unseen world, coming against the power of evil spirits and calling on the authority of the Holy Spirit, will we be effective in healing evangelism.

The same Christ who triumphed over the *lubaale* is able to triumph over spirits of infirmity through your ministry.

We Wrestle Against Principalities and Powers

Ugandans can readily identify with the viewpoint of the apostle Paul, who acknowledged our struggle "against the rulers, against the authorities, against the powers of this dark world and against the spiritual forces of evil in the heavenly realms" (Ephesians 6:12). Ugandans are on the front lines of this conflict, just as the Ephesians, to whom those words were written, were on the front lines in their conflict with the occult worship of Diana or Artemis (Acts 19).

There are several things in particular we in the West can do.

Be Aware of Satan's Schemes

This viewpoint is difficult for many Americans to swallow—even American Christians. Not only do we not believe in the powers of the dark world, we do not even believe in the "heavenly realms" these powers inhabit. We assume that God is far away in a distant heaven while we live on planet earth, ruled by physical (not spiritual) forces; and in between is a lot of empty space. We do not believe that this so-called empty space constitutes the heavenly realms occupied by invisible, warring good and evil angels whose activities strongly influence our daily lives. Even if we acknowledge the existence of heavenly warfare *someplace*, we certainly do not believe that our prayers make any difference in the warfare and its effects on our lives.

It is significant that Paul addressed the following to the Corinthians: "We are not unaware of [Satan's] schemes" (2 Corinthians 2:11). He certainly could not have written that to Americans! We have often been unaware of Satan's schemes and have not even known that a war was going on.

The situation is improving, of course. A few years ago many Christians began to be aware of the war and started praying for nations and against the territorial spirits that rule them. Frank Peretti's novels did not start this trend; they rode the crest of the wave. (Daniel 10 gives an interesting glimpse of spiritual battle with the demonic prince who rules Persia or, in today's terminology, Iraq.) Not long after this God-sent trend of warfare praying against the territorial spirits over nations, the spirits over most of the Communist nations lost much of their power. Communism fell and the spirits could no longer prevent the free spread of the Gospel.

A coincidence? I believe it is cause and effect.

The rise of serious warfare prayer among America's Christians encourages me to believe that many of us will soon learn how to pray effectively for the sick, which is one form of warfare praying.

Stand and Pray

There are two key words in the Ephesians 6:10–20 passage on spiritual warfare. The first is *stand,* which appears four times in the NIV. It describes our defensive posture against Satan, who is like a wrestler trying to pin us to the ground.

The second is *pray*. Alas, many who preach on this passage end at verse 17 and miss the most important part. The key offensive tactic appears several times in the next few verses:

- *Pray,* verse 18
- *Prayers,* verse 18
- *Requests,* verse 18
- *Praying,* verse 18
- *Pray,* verse 19
- *Pray,* verse 20

We are told four times in verses 10–17 to "stand" but six times in the next three verses to "pray." By standing we keep Satan from defeating us. By praying we defeat him.

My brothers and sisters in Uganda understand this. I am praying that more in America will.

What About the Word?

Some may disagree that prayer is our offensive weapon in spiritual warfare. They insist that the Word is, and they have a point. It is by the preaching of the Word that people are converted and the Kingdom of God advanced. The Word is also used offensively to push back the kingdom of Satan. But we are preaching to those who are "dead in . . . transgressions and sins" (Ephesians 2:1) and have been blinded by "the god of this age" (2 Corinthians 4:4). The preaching of God is powerful when it is backed up with prayer.

Some say that the Word is our *only* offensive weapon. They cite Jesus' quotations of Scripture to rebut the devil's temptations in the wilderness (Matthew 4:1–11; Mark 1:12–13; Luke 4:1–13). But this should not be seen as divorced from prayer. It was preceded by forty days of fasting, which certainly included prayer. We should not try to tear apart the Word and prayer. Prayer must be according to Scripture, and any use of Scripture should be supported by prayer.

While they are closely connected, however, each has its own use. Ephesians 6 speaks of praying offensively in spiritual warfare and mentions the Word in connection with the defensive armor that enables us to stand. It is significant that, in the wilderness temptations mentioned above, Jesus quotes Scripture defensively, to protect Himself from Satan's temptations, rather than offensively, to defeat Satan.

I am not trying to minimize the importance of the Word, of course, but rather to show the necessity of offensive prayer in our warfare. Are not some Christians secure (even smug) in their biblical orthodoxy, able to quote Scripture at length yet weak and shallow in prayer? Such persons may insist we are not to use prayer offensively because it is sufficient to quote the Word. But in so doing they betray their own failure to understand the role of prayer in spiritual warfare.

In Ephesians 6, as we have just seen, Paul told us that our defensive posture must be "Stand, stand, stand," and our offensive activity must be "Pray, pray, pray."

Warfare Prayer and Authority over Satan

Why is prayer important in spiritual warfare? Why doesn't God just zap Satan and be done with him? Why do our prayers make any difference in what God does about the enemy?

The same principle applies to spiritual warfare that applies to God's blessings. While God is eager to bless us, He often withholds blessings until we ask for them. He ties His giving to our asking, which releases His power to give.

When God created Adam, He gave him authority to "rule over the fish of the sea and the birds of the air and over every living creature that moves on the ground" (Genesis 1:28). Adam's naming of all the creatures was an expression of this authority (Genesis 2:20). But Adam and Eve turned and, by disobeying God, gave their authority to Satan. Satan is now "the god of this age" (2 Corinthians 4:4) and "the ruler of the kingdom of the air" (Ephesians 2:2). It was not God who gave authority to Satan; it was human beings. And human beings must take it back.

We have already seen in chapter 2 that Jesus gave authority to His disciples. When they noted that evil spirits obeyed them, He explained, "I have given you authority to trample on snakes and scorpions and to overcome all the power of the enemy; nothing will harm you" (Luke 10:19).

"The reason the Son of God appeared," wrote the apostle John, "was to destroy the devil's work" (1 John 3:8). But Jesus does not destroy it all directly. He uses His people. So Paul wrote to the Christians at Rome, "The God of peace will soon crush Satan under your feet" (Romans 16:20). God crushes Satan and uses us and our feet to crush him.

God gave authority to Adam, and Adam gave it to Satan. Jesus gave authority to His people so that we might take back from Satan the authority that Adam wrongly gave him. We do this by prayer.

Warfare Prayer in Healing Evangelism

When you prepare to do healing evangelism, recognize that you are entering combat. Before walking into the meeting where you expect healing evangelism to take place, take authority privately over all unclean spirits that might be present. Bind their power in the name of Jesus, forbid them from hindering your work and serve them notice that they will have to loose persons who have been in bondage to them (see Matthew 18:18).

Sometimes opportunities for healing evangelism arise unexpectedly, as one did for the disciples waiting for Jesus, Peter, James and John to come down from the Mount of Transfiguration. Those disciples had been ineffective in casting a demon out of a boy because of a lack in their prayer lives (Mark 9:29). Jesus could not have expected them to pray about this encounter in advance because it came up suddenly, but at the very time they were being approached by the father of the demonized boy, they were missing an important prayer meeting on the mountain. I doubt that Jesus would have rebuked them for their prayerlessness unless they had been invited to the mountaintop and chosen to stay behind, or unless the lack in their prayer lives disqualified them from an invitation in the first place. In any case, we need to keep "prayed up" so that we have the spiritual strength necessary when emergency situations arise.

When engaging in healing prayer, rebuke spirits of infirmity specifically as Jesus did (Mark 9:25). Break their power and command them to loose their victims. You might pray something like this:

> In the name of Jesus I take authority over all spirits present that are not of Him. I particularly rebuke you spirits of infirmity and command you to loose your victims. By the power of the blood of Christ I command you to depart and go where Jesus sends you. I invite the healing power of the Holy Spirit to burn out all impurity and set this child of God free.

As you launch your ministry of healing evangelism, go in the knowledge that Christ has already won the victory over dark powers and has given you the authority over them, too. Go confident and expectant of victories. These victories come by the power of the Spirit, and that power comes in answer to prayer.

The following chapter will teach you how to pray in the power of the Spirit so as to receive His power for healing.

8

Tapping the Power of the Lord through Prayer

I participated actively in a crusade in Uganda conducted by a healing evangelist from another country whose personality and theology, in part, I found odd. But I was amazed at the remarkable healing miracles the Lord performed through him. I know he spent every day in Uganda praying and fasting, coming out only to preach, and the Lord honored his prayer life with great power for healing.

There is biblical precedent, of course, for the connection between prayer and effective ministry. We saw in the last chapter that the disciples who were not "prayed up" were unable to cast the demon out of the boy. Luke wrote, moreover, that "Jesus often withdrew to lonely places and prayed" (5:16). And in the very next verse, writing about a particular day in Jesus' ministry: "And the power of the Lord was present for him to heal the sick" (5:17). Luke reported on another occasion that "Jesus went out into the hills to pray, and spent the night praying to God" (6:12). Concerning the very next day Luke wrote, "Power was coming from him and healing them all" (6:19).

Do you see a connection between the before and the after? If Jesus needed to spend long hours in prayer in order to receive the power to practice healing evangelism, how much more do we need to pray in the power of the Spirit to receive power for healing?

In this chapter—one of the most important chapters in this book—I want to summarize biblical teaching on the work of the Holy Spirit in our prayers and how to tap the source of power.

Praying in the Spirit

Since healing evangelism is spiritual warfare, and since the key offensive weapon in spiritual warfare (as we saw in the last chapter) is prayer, we should try to understand and practice all that the Scripture teaches us about prayer in the Spirit.

First let's go back to the familiar passage on spiritual warfare that we looked at in the last chapter. "Pray in the Spirit," Paul tells us in Ephesians 6:18, a verse that describes our offensive activity in spiritual warfare. Specifically:

> Pray in the Spirit on all occasions with all kinds of prayers and requests. With this in mind, be alert and always keep on praying for all the saints.

We usually pay little attention when Paul says we are to pray "in the Spirit." After all, we reason, all Christian prayer is in the Holy Spirit, isn't it? Paul's phrase here must be a pious redundancy.

We need to take another look. There are times when even Christians "say" prayers without praying in the Spirit. Making speeches to God or praying to impress others

(Matthew 6:5) and filling the air with meaningless repetition (Matthew 6:7) are examples that many of us, if we are honest, can identify with at one point or another.

But Paul is doing more than urge us not to pray non-prayers. There is special significance in the phrase *in the Spirit*. Paul is talking about warfare against evil spirits and urging us to engage in this warfare with all the power, resources and anointing that the Holy Spirit gives.

He also tells us to "be alert." Why? Because, in Peter's words, "your enemy the devil prowls around like a roaring lion looking for someone to devour" (1 Peter 5:8). We must be on our guard against him constantly, ready to join into battle and to "stand." We need all the help of the Holy Spirit available to us.

Our Western, humanistic worldview causes difficulties for us here. We may find it hard to believe in the reality of evil spirits, or at least their relevance to our daily lives. Likewise, with our anti-supernaturalistic bias, we may find it hard to believe that even the Holy Spirit has much relevance to our lives. As Trinitarians we believe in the Holy Spirit, of course, but He does not fit easily into our rationalistic, materialistic way of looking at life around us.

We need to become alert and wise to the resources of the Holy Spirit. We must cultivate the knowledge and experience of praying with all the anointing and help of the Spirit.

Although most of us read the phrase *in the Spirit* with an interpretation that is bland, vague and only minimally supernatural, others react in the opposite direction. They tell us that whenever the Bible talks about praying "in the Spirit," it is talking only about praying in tongues. These well-meaning brothers and sisters fail to see that Paul is calling on us to use *all* the weapons in the Holy Spirit's arsenal, and not just one of them—a minor one, judging from Paul's prioritized list in 1 Corinthians 12:28—as we engage evil spirits in prayer warfare.

They base their view on Paul's use of the phrase *pray with my spirit* (or *pray with the Spirit*) in the following passage:

> If I pray in a tongue, my spirit prays, but my mind is unfruitful. So what shall I do? I will pray with my spirit, but I will also pray with my mind; I will sing with my spirit, but I will also sing with my mind.
>
> 1 Corinthians 14:14–15

Paul is using the phrase *pray with my spirit* to refer to praying in tongues. But it is important to notice that he is contrasting praying with the Spirit with praying with understanding. Thus, when Paul refers to tongues as "praying with the spirit," he means "praying with the spirit alone." He prefers praying with understanding. But he does not favor praying with the understanding alone over praying with the spirit alone. There is a way of praying with the spirit alone, and that way is tongues. There is also a way, he says, of praying with both the spirit and the mind (1 Corinthians 14:15).

So Paul's teaching of praying "in the Spirit" in Ephesians 6:18 cannot be understood exclusively as praying in the Spirit alone, without understanding. Tongues are one way of praying in the Spirit, of course, and Ephesians 6 urges us to use "all kinds of prayers and requests" (verse 18). So tongues are included. But they are not all.

If I do not know what I am praying, how can I know that I have prayed "all kinds of prayers and requests"? How can I know I have prayed "for all the saints" (verse 18)? More than tongues are included in praying "in the Spirit."

Let's look at some specific ways the Spirit enables us to pray so that we can pray "in the Spirit," especially when we are engaged in the warfare of healing prayer.

With the Spirit of Sonship

"How can I come to God in prayer? He is the supreme, holy, almighty, sovereign God of the universe. I am just one of His creatures made of dust—a worm, a terrible sinner. How can I stand before Him? I should be groveling in shame at His feet. It would be wrong to bother Him about my needs."

You have probably felt like that at times. Most of us have. The Bible's answer is in Romans 8:15–16:

> For you did not receive a spirit that makes you a slave again to fear, but you received the Spirit of sonship. And by him we cry, "*Abba*, Father." The Spirit himself testifies with our spirit that we are God's children.

And in Galatians 4:4–7:

> But when the time had fully come, God sent his Son, born of a woman, born under law, to redeem those under law, that we might receive the full rights of sons. Because you are sons, God sent the Spirit of his Son into our hearts, the Spirit who calls out, "*Abba*, Father." So you are no longer a slave, but a son; and since you are a son, God has made you also an heir.

The Spirit does more than convict you of sin, regenerate you and bring you to faith in Christ. Once you are in Christ, He speaks to your human spirit and assures you that you are God's child with all the rights and privileges that entails. But He does more than that. He puts into your spirit a spirit of sonship, so that you can approach God confidently, freely, as a son or daughter and not as a slave or condemned criminal.

A boy waits by the window for his father to return home from work. Finally he sees him coming up the walk. He runs from the house, throws his arms around his father's legs and cries, "Daddy, Daddy, Daddy!" He is showing not disrespect but love. He knows the greatness of his father, but he also knows his privilege as a son.

A child from another home will not approach this man in the same familiar way. But because of this boy's special relationship of sonship, he has both freedom and boldness in his access to his parent.

In Paul's day, *Abba* was the equivalent of our *Daddy*. Paul says that the Holy Spirit enables you to cry, "Daddy!" in the same way that Jesus cried out to His Father—because you are God's child through Christ.

Many who are truly God's sons and daughters have not fully experienced the spirit of sonship. They still have a spirit of fear and bondage before God. They need to allow the Holy Spirit to witness to their spirits in such a way that the spirit of fear is taken away and replaced with the spirit that cries, "Daddy!"

If ordinary prayer requires the assurance of sonship, how much more does healing prayer! We need the Spirit to assure us not only of our sonship, but of our special rights and privileges as sons and daughters to rebuke spirits of infirmity, take authority over disease and minister healing in the name of Christ. Our healing prayers are not likely to be specific, bold, believing and effective until we gain this assurance.

With the Seal of the Holy Spirit

Paul talks of the Holy Spirit as a seal or deposit in the following passages:

> He anointed us, set his seal of ownership on us, and put his Spirit in our hearts as a deposit, guaranteeing what is to come.
>
> 2 Corinthians 1:21–22

It is God who has made us for this very purpose and has given us the Spirit as a deposit, guaranteeing what is to come.

2 Corinthians 5:5

Having believed [in Christ], you were marked in him with a seal, the promised Holy Spirit, who is a deposit guaranteeing our inheritance until the redemption of those who are God's possession—to the praise of his glory.

Ephesians 1:13–14

Do not grieve the Holy Spirit of God, with whom you were sealed for the day of redemption.

Ephesians 4:30

A person who buys a home makes a deposit of earnest money to show that he or she intends to pay the full purchase price. We are not in heaven yet, but God has given us a down payment by placing the Holy Spirit in our hearts. He is the deposit or earnest, the sign that we will receive our complete redemption in heaven.

But the Spirit as a seal or deposit is not just a concept we have to take on faith; He is to be felt. Many Scriptures indicate this, including:

Hope does not disappoint us, because God has poured out his love into our hearts by the Holy Spirit, whom he has given us.

Romans 5:5

Though you have not seen [Christ], you love him; and even though you do not see him now, you believe in him and are filled with an inexpressible and glorious joy.

1 Peter 1:8

Some prefer a religion that is formal, academic and cerebral. They object to the concept of a Christianity that can be felt. And since the assurance of regeneration clearly comes *after* regeneration, and since many do not receive that assurance until much later, they dismiss the sealing as "second blessing-ism." But the sealing is not a second blessing divorced from the first; it is the strong assurance that the first has taken place.

There are, of course, many blessings in the Christian life. It is sad that some want none but the first.

Those who object say, "The sealing of the Holy Spirit is positional rather than experiential truth. It is not something we experience but something we believe. The Father puts a seal, as it were, on the forehead of every true believer, invisible to us but visible to Him, so He knows the believer is His son or daughter whom He must keep secure."

But the Father already knows that I am His. He does not need to mark my forehead to remind Him to keep me secure! If I buy your house and give you earnest money as a sign of my commitment to show up at settlement and make the final payment, is the deposit a sign to me or to you? To you, of course. A deposit is a sign to the receiver, not the giver. In the same way, the Holy Spirit is a sign not to the Father who gives Him, but to us who receive Him. As such He must be experienced.

Many Christians today have "syllogistic assurance." They reason like this:

- All who believe in Christ are saved.
- I believe in Christ.
- Therefore, I am saved.

Syllogistic assurance is good, but it is only a beginning. You need more than a syllogism; you need a seal—the seal of the Holy Spirit.

My friend the late Dr. D. Martyn Lloyd Jones tells a wonderful story in *Joy Unspeakable*, his book on the sealing with the Holy Spirit, that he learned from the writings of an old Puritan theologian, Thomas Goodwin.

He relates that a father and son are walking along hand in hand. The son knows that his father loves him, cares for him and protects him. Is his father not right now holding his hand? But suddenly, as they walk along, the father stops, picks up his son, covers his face with kisses and says, "My son, I love you, I love you, I love you!"

Walking along hand in hand is ordinary Christian assurance. Being picked up and covered with kisses is the sealing with the Holy Spirit!

Please do not be content with ordinary Christian assurance. The first and most basic aspect of praying in the Holy Spirit is to approach the Father freely with the Spirit of His Son crying in your heart, "Daddy, Daddy, Daddy!" You need to pray with this spirit to be effective in healing prayer.

With the Spirit of Groaning

Have you ever had the following experience?

You are praying about something you feel deeply about. You know it is something God also feels deeply about. Perhaps you are praying about some human misery, or about people who are lost, or about tribes that are unreached with the Gospel. As you express your burden to the Lord, you are aware that He is giving you something of His own burden on the subject. As you pray, you sense that the Spirit is sighing or groaning to the Father from inside you. God by His Spirit is giving you something of His heart of compassion on the matter. Finally you run out of words, stop talking and rest. But you are aware that deep down inside you the Spirit is continuing to pray and groan.

Paul describes this experience in Romans 8:26–27:

> In the same way, the Spirit helps us in our weakness. We do not know what we ought to pray, but the Spirit himself intercedes for us with groans that words cannot express. And he who searches our hearts knows the mind of the Spirit, because the Spirit intercedes for the saints in accordance with God's will.

Some people think this passage is about tongues (just as some think the Ephesians admonition about praying in the Spirit refers only to tongues). But if it were, Paul would have said, "The Spirit helps you pray in a heavenly language that you do not understand." Instead he said that the Spirit does the praying with groans and no words at all.

This passage describes two different but related ways the Holy Spirit prays within you. One is with groanings that give feeling and fervency to your prayers. This is what I described just now. The other way is by speaking your prayers to the Father and expressing them more perfectly than you can.

When I preach in a foreign country and do not know the local language, I preach through an interpreter. The translator takes my message phrase by phrase and puts the English in a language the people understand. So it is that the Spirit takes our prayers and utters them perfectly in the hearing of the Father. We often do not know what the will of the Lord is, so we ask imperfectly. The Spirit takes our imperfect prayers and speaks them so that the Father hears them correctly.

For years my wife, Eileen, had kidney stones and did not know it. That was remarkable, since kidney stones usually cause excruciating pain. All she had was a frequent low-grade fever, which we assumed was a recurrence of malaria. So for years I urged people to pray for my wife's malaria. But, as we believe now, the Spirit was taking the prayers of our Christian brothers and sisters about Eileen's malaria and saying, "Father, they're really praying about her kidney stones. Don't let them hurt her!" They did *not* hurt her and, even though Eileen still has them (they have been greatly reduced in size by lithotripsy), they are still not hurting her.

What is it to pray "in the Spirit"? It means to have the Spirit pray in you, unite His prayers to yours and give you a measure of His own fervent spirit on the subject. It means that you receive a spirit of sonship that enables you to pray with confidence in your position and rights as a child of God. It means that your prayers are anointed and empowered by the Spirit and by His prayers. It means that you are enabled to pray with a measure of the compassion of God as it is poured into your heart by the Spirit.

Praying in the Spirit is cooperating with the Spirit in prayer. He anoints your prayers, gives you fervency and groans in prayer right along with you.

Be Filled with the Holy Spirit

Jesus Christ arose from the dead on Easter morning. That evening He met with His disciples and "breathed on them and said, 'Receive the Holy Spirit'" (John 20:22).

Throughout the Gospel of John we read promises of the coming of the Spirit:

> Whoever drinks the water I give him will never thirst. Indeed, the water I give him will become in him a spring of water welling up to eternal life.
>
> John 4:14

> If a man is thirsty, let him come to me and drink. Whoever believes in me, as the Scripture has said, streams of living water will flow from within him.
>
> John 7:37–38

> I will ask the Father, and he will give you another Counselor to be with you forever—the Spirit of truth. . . . You know him, for he lives with you and will be in you.
>
> John 14:16–17

Christ's breathing on the disciples on Easter Sunday night was the fulfillment of these promises. Before that night He was with them, but after that night He indwelt them and every believer.

But there was more to come. Jesus later said to the disciples:

> Do not leave Jerusalem, but wait for the gift my Father promised, which you have heard me speak about. For John baptized with water, but in a few days you will be baptized with the Holy Spirit. . . . You will receive power when the Holy Spirit comes on you; and you will be my witnesses in Jerusalem, and in all Judea and Samaria, and to the ends of the earth.
>
> Acts 1:4–5, 8

This magnificent promise was fulfilled on the day of Pentecost in the amazing events recorded in Acts 2, when "all of them were filled with the Holy Spirit" (verse 4).

How do we relate the events of Easter Sunday night with those of Pentecost?

- On Easter the disciples *received* the Holy Spirit; on Pentecost they were *filled* with the Holy Spirit.
- On Easter the Holy Spirit came *into* them; on Pentecost He overflowed *onto* them with power and authority.
- On Easter they received the Holy Spirit and received the *potential* for all the gifts and power of the Spirit within them; on Pentecost, when they were filled with

the Spirit, they received the *actual* gifts and power of the Spirit for witness unto the ends of the earth.

- On Easter they received the Person of the Spirit *without* any manifestations of His gifts and power; on Pentecost they received Him *with* immediate manifestations of His gifts and power, beginning with the gift of tongues.

Many Christians today remind me of the disciples between Easter night and Pentecost. They have received Christ and have the indwelling Spirit, but are not yet filled with the Spirit. The gifts and power of the Spirit are within them potentially but are not yet released.

Pray in the Spirit for Power for Healing

We have already seen that when we engage in healing evangelism, we are confronting the power of the enemy. For this combat, and for effective healing evangelism, we need all the power of the Holy Spirit. We need to pray "in the Spirit" as I have described above; to be indwelt, assured, sealed and filled with the Holy Spirit; and to pray with all the resources the Holy Spirit gives us.

If ever there is a time when we need to use "all kinds of prayers and requests" (Ephesians 6:18), it is when we are doing healing evangelism! This means we need the gifts of the Spirit, including the manifestational gifts of 1 Corinthians 12, which are particularly appropriate for healing prayer. Some people say these gifts are not for today, and that we should not seek to receive and utilize them. But if we want to engage in healing evangelism, we will then be going into battle with only a small portion of the equipment the Lord has for us.

We discuss these gifts in the next chapter—and, in the chapter after that, the openness to the Spirit that is necessary for the reception and operation of the gifts.

9

"Lord, Stop the Rain!"

Peterson Sozi had reserved a campsite on Lake Victoria in Uganda and invited his entire congregation to join him there for a week of prayer and fasting to seek the mind of the Lord. When the week ended they believed that God had indeed met with them and showed them that they were to go to the town of Mbale and hold a weeklong evangelistic crusade. At the end of the week they would be able to plant a church.

The Mbale crusade began on a Monday from an open-air platform constructed on a cricket ground—a natural gathering place. The songs and testimonies of the evangelistic team, accompanied by electric guitars and keyboard and amplified by loudspeakers, drew good crowds. Peterson preached strong sermons urging the people to repent and come back to God through Jesus Christ.

During Wednesday's rally something remarkable happened that I later heard on an audiocassette tape. Peterson was calling on those who would repent to come to the front to be led in a prayer of repentance. People started forward. Suddenly it began to rain. Because this was the rainy season on the equator, it was no light drizzle but a torrential, tropical downpour. When such rains come they last not a few minutes but a few hours. Clearly audible on the tape is the sound of rain pelting the nylon sheet that had been placed over the tape recorder for protection.

This can't be from the Lord, Peterson thought (as he told me later). *Not now, just as people are getting saved.*

So he called in a loud voice, amplified over the sound system, "Lord, stop the rain!"

Instantly the rain stopped. The sound on the cassette tape of rain pounding on the nylon sheet ends abruptly and you can hear the crowd burst into spontaneous applause.

Word got around Mbale quickly about the God of the evangelists who could stop the rain. Some of the townspeople went home and to the hospitals to bring their sick to the rally for prayer the next day. And from Thursday on there were very large crowds, miraculous healings and many professions of faith.

On Sunday, the last day of the crusade week, a meeting in the morning constituted the first service of the new church. A large crowd joined the church that first Sunday, most of them new converts from the crusade. In addition, the Full Gospel Church in Mbale, along with its pastor, dissolved and joined the new Mbale Presbyterian Church.

That church in Mbale was established by healing evangelism and by what might be called miracle evangelism. The crusade had been made effective by many gifts of the Spirit, including the working of miracles.

We have already seen that Christ came into the world to destroy the devil's work. He not only preached the Kingdom of God but pushed back the kingdom of Satan by calling people to repentance, healing the sick and casting out demons. He gave power to His disciples to do the same things. Before He ascended to heaven He told them to teach everything He had commanded them, which included driving out evil spirits and healing diseases.

We have also seen that, as we prayerfully engage the forces of darkness, we need to utilize all the resources of the Holy Spirit, including the gifts of the Spirit—and especially the manifestational gifts, or so-called "sign gifts," of 1 Corinthians 12:8–10. These gifts are invaluable in prayer, particularly when we are ministering to others in healing evangelism. Let's take a look at them.

The Manifestational Gifts

Paul's teaching on manifestational gifts appears in a section of a letter devoted to a discussion of what happens when the church gathers.

What Are They?

The nine manifestational gifts listed in 1 Corinthians 12: 8–10 can be viewed in three sets as follows:

- *Word Gifts*: words of wisdom and words of knowledge
- *Power Gifts*: faith, healing, miracles, prophecy and discernment of spirits
- *Language Gifts*: tongues and interpretation

Word gifts help us know how to pray and what to pray for. Power gifts pertain to the effective results of our prayers. Language gifts relate specifically to praying in unknown languages and understanding the meaning of those prayers.

When Do We Use Them?

The treatment of gifts appears in a larger context of issues that arise when the Church is gathered. From that larger context we conclude that the gifts may be utilized:

- In your meetings (11:17)
- When you come together (11:18)
- When you come together (11:20)
- When you come together (11:33)
- For the common good (12:7)
- In the church (12:28)
- In the church (14:19)
- If the whole church comes together (14:23)
- When you come together (14:26)

How Do They Work?

On one occasion when the church is gathered (in whatever form, including home groups), you may get a word of wisdom. Someone may get a gift of healing for your bad back. Your wife may get a gift of healing for someone else's stomach problem. The following week your wife may get a gift of healing for someone's poor eyesight. Someone else may get a word of wisdom. You may get nothing at all. The gifts are temporary and distributed by the sovereign Spirit as they are needed in the assembly on each particular occasion. All gifts are available to all believers, each at the time it is needed and only at that time.

Normally these gifts do not occur when we are listening to a sermon, but during prayer ministry, and they have special relevance when we are ministering in healing prayer.

Many err by viewing them as permanent gifts for each individual. They think that if you have a gift for one moment, you have it forever. There are evangelists who claim "the gift of healing," even though Scripture speaks of "gifts" (plural) of healing. I take this to mean that there is not one gift of forever being a mighty healing evangelist. Nor does receiving a word of wisdom mean that you are forever wise. Words of wisdom are temporary; once spoken, they are gone. No, it is more biblical to see the gifts as episodic, transitory—gifts the Spirit gives as and when they are needed.

It is true that "God's gifts and his call are irrevocable" (Romans 11:29). That these gifts do not last forever in an individual's experience is not that God has taken them back but that they are, by their very nature, brief. If I give you one hundred dollars and you spend it, then you no longer have it, but not because I have taken it back. Once you speak a word of wisdom or knowledge or prophecy, it is spent. God does not revoke any gift, but these gifts are intended to manifest the immediate activity of the Holy Spirit. Once each manifestation has taken place, we must await new manifestations to be expressed in new gifts.

How Do They Work in Healing Prayer?

Here are examples of how each of the nine manifestational gifts may be used in connection with healing evangelism:

As you pray for direction in counseling an individual with emotional hurts, a thought occurs to you that seems very wise. You counsel the individual accordingly, and he or she agrees it is a wise solution to the problem. The Lord has given you a *word of wisdom.*

As you are praying for a man with ulcers, it occurs to you to ask, "Could these ulcers be due to problems with your wife?" You may not even have known he is married. He is amazed you knew to suggest this, tells you he is under great strain in his marriage and agrees this may well be the cause of the ulcers. As you pray for the healing of his ulcers, you also pray for the healing of his marriage.

You have received a *word of knowledge* that enables you to pray more accurately.

As you are praying for a particular healing, you receive strong inward confirmation that what you are asking for is indeed the will of the Lord and that He will do it. This enables you to pray with more confidence and forcefulness. Soon the healing comes. You have received a gift of *faith.*

You are praying for someone with a migraine. As you pray, the migraine suddenly disappears. You have received a gift of *healing.*

You are holding an open-air evangelistic rally and people are starting to respond to the Gospel, when it begins to pour rain. Stopping the rain on command, as Peterson did, is an example of a gift of *miraculous power.*

In a church service with unbelievers present, you are led to stand up and say, "There is a man here who has a wife and three children. He is having an adulterous affair and is considering leaving his family. That man must repent." An unbeliever you have never seen stands up and admits in astonishment that you have just described him. He immediately repents and receives Christ (see 1 Corinthians 14:24–25). You have spoken a *word of prophecy.*

You are praying for a woman with suicidal tendencies. She says she hears voices in her head telling her to kill herself. You discern that she is in bondage to evil spirits. The names of these spirits are given to you. One is *Suicide* and the other is *Lust*. You command them to leave in the name of Jesus, and the woman you are praying for senses that something has indeed left. (She has experienced deliverance but will need further counseling). You have received a gift of *discernment.*

You are praying with a person for healing and waiting quietly on God, not sure how to pray. In your mind you sense foreign words that you do not understand and you are sure they were given you by the Holy Spirit. You speak these words in prayer and soon the healing comes. The Holy Spirit knew just what to ask. You have experienced a gift of a *different kind of tongue.*

As you are praying in tongues, you sense what you are praying about. You do not have an exact translation, because the things you are saying are "mysteries" beyond your complete comprehension (1 Corinthians 14:2), but you have a general sense of the nature of your prayer. You have received a gift of *interpretation.*

More About Tongues

Because there is much misunderstanding today on the nature of tongues and interpretation, I want to give them further consideration.

"Is It Really Important?"

That is the way I often answer when someone asks me if I speak in tongues. The Christian world is divided between two warring parties, each of which thinks of tongues as extremely important. One party says that a person who has never spoken in tongues has not been filled with the Holy Spirit. The other party says that those who speak in tongues are under demonic delusion and should be regarded, no matter how orthodox they may be about Christ, as belonging to the lunatic heretical fringe along with Mormons, Moonies and Jehovah's Witnesses.

If the Lord has given me the ability to pray to Him in a heavenly language, isn't that between the Lord and me? Surely it does not make me either a super-Christian or a demonically deceived cultist.

For twenty years I pastored churches, none of which was charismatic. When I made calls to visitors to the church, a few would tell me they spoke in tongues, then watch to see my reaction. Would I have a stroke or fit or fainting spell? Would I fly into a rage? Would I welcome them to a secret society working to charismaticize the congregation?

"One of the things I get from reading 1 Corinthians 12–14," I would respond, "is that tongues are not worth hassling over. Most of the people in our church don't speak in tongues, but I don't think they'll hassle you because you do. I hope you won't hassle them because they don't."

Some of these visitors I never heard from again. Perhaps some went on to other churches that would allow them to hassle. Others joined our church and enriched our fellowship.

Tongues in the Bible

Here are facts about speaking in tongues that I have gleaned from the Bible:

Tongues-speaking is offering prayers addressed to God. "Anyone who speaks in a tongue," wrote Paul, "does not speak to men but to God. Indeed, no one understands him; he utters mysteries with his spirit" (1 Corinthians 14:2).

Tongues are for private prayer. "I thank God that I speak in tongues more than all of you," wrote Paul. "But in the church I would rather speak five intelligible words to instruct others than ten thousand words in a tongue" (1 Corinthians 14:18–19). Paul spoke often in tongues, but not in church. His tongues were used in his private prayer times.

The tongues of Acts 2 were not *known human languages unknown to the speakers.* Many have concluded otherwise from a superficial study of the passage, which points out that the languages were heard as known human languages. But a close study reveals a miracle of speaking plus miracles of hearing. When the 120 were filled with the Spirit they all spoke in tongues. Visitors from Egypt heard them all speaking Egyptian; those from Libya heard them all speaking Libyan; those from Rome heard them all speaking Roman; and so forth (Acts 2:4–13). Many hearers were given the miraculous ability to hear all of them praising God, each in his own native language.

Some present were mockers, however, who received no miracle of hearing. How did the tongues sound to *them,* who heard the words spoken without miraculous interference? "They have had too much wine," they said (verse 13).

I conclude that we are not to expect tongues always to be known human languages, but more often to sound like the meaningless babble of drunks. We hear stories of people in modern times who have heard messages in their mother languages spoken by others who have not learned these languages. Perhaps in these instances, too, miracles of hearing have been granted.

Tongues may be angelic languages. Paul, in the middle of his discourse on speaking in tongues, wrote, "If I speak in the tongues of men and of angels. . . " (1 Corinthians 13:1). Thus, we cannot always expect tongues to conform to the patterns of human language.

Nothing in Scripture suggests that speaking in tongues is "automatic" speech. Some describe their initial experience of tongues as if they were suddenly, involuntarily speaking words they did not understand, giving the appearance that tongues-speaking is a mechanical process bypassing the brain. Others, however, speak of strange words in their minds that they feel led voluntarily to speak. Tongues do *not* bypass the brain; they come through the brain. Often, however, they come so rapidly that they seem almost automatic. We speak as the Spirit gives the words (Acts 2:4). They may come to you in much the same way as a name you have forgotten may suddenly come to mind.

Tongues-speakers are probably not in a state of ecstasy, nor are their actions out of control. When you read aloud from a book, you are in perfect control of what and how you are speaking, although you are not choosing your own words. They are selected for you by the words on the page. In the same way, a tongues-speaker is in complete control of his speech, except that he is not choosing his own words. They are being chosen for him by the Holy Spirit. He voluntarily speaks the words the Holy Spirit puts in his mind even though he does not understand them. He controls the volume, speed, intonation and everything else except the words, which are given to him.

Tongues are for all believers, not just the "super-spiritual." Jesus lists tongues among the signs that will follow all believers (Mark 16:17).

Tongues are to be discouraged from use in public church services. There may be no more than three utterances and never without interpretation (1 Corinthians 14:27).

The fruit of the Spirit (Galatians 5:22–23) is more important than the gifts of the Spirit. Without the fruit the gifts are worthless (1 Corinthians 13). God will judge us for our sanctification, not our gifts. Those with gifts and without sanctification will be rejected (Matthew 7:21–23).

The gift of tongues is the least of the gifts. We may infer this from the listing of gifts in 1 Corinthians 12:27–31, in which tongues and interpretation of tongues are placed last. Tongues are the one gift for personal edification and not for the Church (1 Corinthians 14:4). That this is the least of the gifts may help us understand why it is often the first gift some believers receive. It is easier to pray in a tongue than pray effectively for the sick or cast out demons. It is a good place for the novice to begin.

Tongues can be very useful in the spiritual warfare aspect of healing evangelism. Once in Africa I was attempting to cast out a demon. It was stubborn and difficult to dislodge. I prayed many things in English that were ineffective. Then I prayed out loud in a tongue. The demon growled at me angrily and suddenly was gone. I do not know what I said but apparently the demon did. In any case, the Holy Spirit gave me just the words needed to drive out this spirit. (Ephesians 6:18 says to use all kinds of prayer in warfare. That includes tongues.)

Receiving the Gifts

If you believe in Christ, you have the Holy Spirit living in you (Romans 8:9). Because He is in you, all the power and gifts of the Spirit are potentially in you as well. Jesus gave the Holy Spirit to indwell believers on Easter Sunday night, as we saw in chapter 8. Days later at Pentecost, believers were filled from within and the gifts and power of the Spirit were released. Many Christians today (as I have said) are like the disciples between Easter and Pentecost. The Spirit is in them but the gifts and power need to be released. Pray that both will be released in your life (see Luke 11:13).

Some people believe that because Jesus told the disciples to "tarry" at Jerusalem (Luke 24:49, KJV; see also Acts 1:4), we must "tarry" in prayer a long time, too, before the Spirit will be released in our lives. But that instruction was given before Pentecost. The Holy Spirit came at Pentecost and never left. He is here. We do not need to wait for Him. After praying, go in faith seeking and expecting the gifts and power to be released in your life. Pray for the sick and the demonized. Seek to manifest other gifts.

The first one likely to come to you is tongues. Ask the Spirit to take control of your mind and drive out all spirits not of Jesus. Then ask the Lord to give you words in an unknown tongue by which you can praise Him. Focus on the Lord, open your mouth and praise Him with whatever words He gives you. Do not pay too much attention to the words and do not be self-conscious. Just praise Him with whatever words He places in your mind and heart.

In the next chapter we will consider the leading of the Spirit that enables us to discern what He intends to do and what gifts He is making available at the moment.

10

"The Lord Just Spoke to Me"

The Lord just spoke to me," announced a believer in an underground church service in Uganda.

"How did He speak to you?" responded a fellow believer playfully. "In English, Swahili or Luganda?"

"I'm serious. The Lord just told me that Amin's soldiers are coming. We must end our prayer meeting and leave here quickly."

This conversation, and many like it, took place in the days when Idi Amin banned churches and ordered his security forces to find illegal services and arrest everyone in them. Often those who were arrested were later killed.

Minutes later the soldiers arrived intent on arresting everyone. No one was there.

God often speaks guidance to individual believers and congregations, even in situations not so dramatic or perilous as Amin's Uganda. How do we know it is He who is speaking? And how can we discern His guidance?

We know that Jesus discerned God's guidance. At the Bethesda pool, for example (as we saw in chapter 3), He saw many sick people but healed only one (John 5:1–15). Later Jesus explained, "I tell you the truth, the Son can do nothing by himself; he can do only what he sees his Father doing, because whatever the Father does the Son also does" (verse 19). Jesus did not attempt to heal everyone. He was sensitive to the leading of the Spirit and did only the things the Father showed Him He wanted to do through Him.

A key to success in healing evangelism, then, is being sensitive to the leading of the Spirit and cooperating with Him in the things He wants to do.

That does not mean we should not pray for someone who requests it if we feel no special leading of the Spirit. The most loving thing we can do for someone is to pray. Often the Lord will heal even when we have no special leading. But our effectiveness in healing evangelism is related directly to our ability to sense what the Spirit wants to do and pray that those things will come to pass.

Questions for the Spirit

We face any number of questions in healing prayer for which we have desperate need for guidance and answers from the Holy Spirit:

When do I pray for the sick and for whom do I pray? Jesus needed to know that God wanted Him to heal just one person at the pool that day.

What method should I use? Should I command a lame person to get up, as Jesus did that day? Or does God want me to anoint the person with oil or perhaps lay hands on him or her?

When I pray, what specifically should I ask? Should I just pray generally for the ability of the person to stand and walk (or whatever)? Perhaps there are particular medical problems that I should address in prayer.

Often there are root problems that need to considered. Stomach disorders may reflect ulcers or anxiety. Other problems may reflect bitterness or unforgiveness in personal relationships. Perhaps the problems are the result of the work of an unclean spirit that must be rebuked and cast out.

What counsel should I give? Should I urge the person to repent of particular sins that have contributed to his or her condition? Should I strongly recommend reconciliation with certain people? Should I assure the person of the forgiveness of Christ and offer him or her hope?

We will be exploring some of these questions in upcoming chapters. But the leading of the Spirit in all of them is essential.

The Leading of the Spirit

Most of us believe in the individual guidance of the Spirit. Believers say, "The Lord spoke to me in my quiet time this morning." Pastors say, "The Lord called me to preach" or "The Lord called me to pastor this church."

Whenever I preach (and I am not unusual in this), I seek to go into the pulpit with a strong sense that God has given me a particular message to preach on this particular occasion. Often as I am preaching, points of application occur to me that I did not think of when preparing the message. I speak these words as if they are part of the prepared sermon even though they are spontaneous messages from the Spirit. Often these are the points the Lord uses most to bring conviction or comfort.

Nor am I alone in believing that the Lord showed me exactly whom I was to marry; and years later I am all the more amazed at the excellence of His wisdom in His choice for me. Many of us believe that the Lord has guided us in our career choices and basic life decisions. We also find the Lord directing us in small daily decisions when we ask Him to.

Those of us who believe that the gifts of the Spirit operate today often speak of these leadings as prophecy, words of wisdom and words of knowledge. Some, including those who believe that other gifts, but not these gifts, operate today, oppose using such terms. They consider these gifts as revelational and know that revelation ceased with the completion of the New Testament. At the other extreme are those who refer to guidance they have received from the Spirit as revelation or revelation knowledge.

Listening to the Lord and following the direction of His Spirit is not easy. There are pitfalls. Some have listened to spirits that were not the Holy Spirit (but they thought they were) and gotten into trouble. False cults have arisen as spirits give new doctrine contrary to the Word of God. Orthodox groups have become cultic as messages not in contradiction to Scripture but in addition to Scripture have been believed and followed. Christians have come into legalistic bondage as rules have been imposed on them by "deceiving spirits" (1 Timothy 4:1–3). Others have been manipulated by domineering people who told them they had messages from God for them.

It is crucial for us to explore the difference between revelation and the present-day leading of the Holy Spirit.

Is It Leading or Is It Revelation?

Discerning the Holy Spirit's leading is a vital element of effective prayer for the sick. Many are hindered at this point because they have confused guidance and revelation. They know that revelation has ceased and that the Scriptures are sufficient. But because they know that the Spirit does not speak new revelation today, they assume that the Spirit must be silent, so they do not listen for His voice.

This confusion limits the effectiveness of many Christians in praying for the sick. So I believe it is vital to take a few pages to clarify the important issues of revelation and the leading of the Spirit.

It is important to understand that revelation has ceased. God's revelation is written in the Bible. It is complete. The Bible contains everything necessary for salvation. It contains all God's will for His Church. It is the story of God's plan of redemption culminating in Christ, who completed redemption on the cross and cried, "It is finished" (John 19:30). When the New Testament message of Christ was complete, we had a finished revelation of a finished redemption.

Listen to the author of Hebrews: "In the past God spoke to our forefathers through the prophets at many times and in various ways, but in these last days he has spoken to us by his Son" (1:1–2). Which is to say, Jesus Christ is God's last word to man. When God gave us His Son, He told us everything. He has revealed everything necessary for salvation and all His will for His Church.

If you think there might be more revelation to add to the Bible, or if you are toying with any kind of extrabiblical teaching, you are saying that Christ and His Gospel are not enough. It is for a reason that the very last page of the Bible says, "I warn everyone who hears the words of the prophecy of this book: If anyone adds anything to them, God will add to him the plagues described in this book" (Revelation 22:18).

God speaks guidance today to individuals and congregations, but His personal messages should not be confused with revelation for His whole Church or for all the world. In its original sense, of course, the word *revelation* can be used of almost any communication from one person to another. Daily I receive "revelations" from my wife and children. However, *revelation* is used by Christians in a precise, technical sense; and guidance from the Spirit should not be confused with this kind of revelation.

We should reject every message contrary to Scripture and, just as important, every message that adds to Scripture by giving new teaching "necessary for salvation" or containing "God's will for His whole Church." When such messages come, we can be sure that the spirits that send them are not the Holy Spirit.

Guidelines for Prophecies

The Holy Spirit does speak guidance to individuals and congregations; we have seen this already. These can variously be called prophecies, words of wisdom and words of knowledge—gifts that are operating today in non-revelational ways.

At the same time we must recognize that no prophecies today come in infallible form. This was true even in New Testament times, but not in the Old Testament. True prophets in the Old Testament spoke infallible words of God, and anyone prophesying something that did not come to pass, or who performed a sign or wonder but used it to try to entice believers in Yahweh to worship other gods, was a false prophet and was to be stoned to death (Deuteronomy 13:1–5; 18:20–22). In New Testament times the apostles took over the ministry of speaking infallible revelation, and the prophets operated on a lower level than they did in the Old Testament. Today prophecies are to be judged (1 Corinthians 14:29). Some, therefore, will be rejected. But those who prophesy inaccurately are not to be put to death.

Prophecies are to be "[weighed] carefully" (1 Corinthians 14:29). When they are spoken in church, others should be given the opportunity to evaluate them. It is best not to give prophecies in the first person as if they are spoken directly by God, I believe, because that discourages evaluation. They are not the infallible speech of God and should not be presented as if they are. Who wants to be in a position to evaluate what God says? Yet it is amazing how many prophecies are spoken in King James English and accompanied by *Thus saith the Lord*. One would think that by now God would have learned to speak in contemporary English! Better to say something like this: "I believe I have a sense of what the Lord wants to say to us today."

Don't write prophecies down. They do not need to be preserved. They are given by God for specific individuals or congregations in specific circumstances and times. Writing them down tempts people to treat them on a par with Scripture.

Don't give a prophecy as if it were an interpretation of a message someone has given in tongues. Your prophecy may be a true prophecy, but if it is, it is not an interpretation of the tongue. Scripture is explicit that "anyone who speaks in a tongue does not speak to men but to God. . . . But everyone who prophesies speaks to men for their strengthening, encouragement and comfort" (1 Corinthians 14:2–3). A true interpretation of a tongue will be a prayer to God, not your word to men. It is not true, as some say, that tongues plus interpretation equals prophecy. No, tongues plus interpretation equals prayer in an understandable language.

Beware of directive prophecies: "God told me to tell you what you are to do." If He has a message for me, why doesn't He tell me Himself? By directive prophecies many domineering persons have manipulated others for their own purposes.

Following the Spirit's Leading

We all agree, I hope, in the sufficiency of Scripture—that God spoke His final word when He told us of Christ and His finished redemption. Most of us also agree that the Spirit continues to speak today, but that these messages are not revelation; they are simply matters of guidance. He told the Ugandan believers when the soldiers were coming. He called many of us into careers, perhaps even into the ministry of preaching His Word. He directs us in our personal prayer times and also when we are praying for the sick.

You may or may not agree with me that these present-day communications of the Spirit are modern, non-revelational forms of the gifts of prophecy, word of wisdom and word of knowledge. You may want to call them simply leadings, guidance or impressions of the Spirit. It is not important what you call them. It *is* important, if you want to be effective in healing evangelism, to develop the spiritual sensitivity necessary to recognize and follow them.

We have been looking in Part 3 at what we need to do healing evangelism—faith, victory in spiritual warfare, power from prayer, the gifts and the guidance of the Spirit. In Part 4 we will be taking a "hands-on" approach to healing evangelism. Often the Spirit will guide us to anoint someone with oil or pray for him or her by laying on our hands. Sometimes He may lead us to command demons to leave. But these practices make some of us uncomfortable.

We will be discussing them in the next chapter.

Part 4

Aspects of Healing Evangelism

Why do healing evangelists anoint with oil and lay on hands? Do they think there is some magic in these gestures? And how do you deliver a person who is tormented by evil spirits or bring healing to a person whose hurt is emotional?

These are the questions we will look at in this section.

11

Oil, Hands and Spit

The little beggar girl in Bombay spurned the rupees I offered her.

"Dollar," she said in her limited English. "Please give me dollar."

The next moment she hurried away happy with the dollar bill I gave her.

That little girl knew not only a little English but something about economics and how to size up a foreign visitor.

Most beggars in Bombay are not so sophisticated. They just stand with sad faces and outstretched palms. Nevertheless, although no word is spoken, I understand clearly what they want, since human beings speak with gestures as well as words.

In prayer, too, we can communicate with gestures. Kneeling, hands outstretched with palms up or hands upraised in praise are not only prayer postures but "gesture prayers" in which we express ourselves to God. The New Testament gives many instances of gesture prayers, or what might be called "action prayers." These are prayers in which some physical action accompanies the words, or perhaps even stands alone as an action without words communicating meaning to God.

These action prayers occur most often in healing evangelism. Indeed, there are few recorded examples of healing that do not include action prayers. Action prayers, for reasons we will consider later in this chapter, are vital for effective healing prayer and are an essential element in healing evangelism.

Action Prayers

Let's look at five of the different kinds of action prayers that are part of prayer for healing.

Anointing with Oil

The first kind of action prayer for healing is anointing with oil. It was a common practice of the disciples (Mark 6:13) and was later required by James for use by church elders in healing services (James 5:14). Anointing with oil is a prayer that the person will be anointed with the healing power of the Holy Spirit. Oil is a frequent symbol of the Holy Spirit in the Scriptures, most obviously in Zechariah 4.

Touch and Spittle

When praying for the sick, Jesus sometimes used a combination of touch and spittle—with the deaf and dumb beggar (Mark 7:33) and with the man blind from birth (John 9:6).

Touch

Many action prayers involve touch. This is the means by which Jesus blessed the children (Mark 10:16) and by which the first-century Church conveyed the power of the Holy Spirit (Acts 8:17; 9:12, 17; 13:3; 19:6).

It was also used commonly for healing:

> Jesus reached out his hand and touched the man. "I am willing," he said. "Be clean!" Immediately he was cured of his leprosy.
>
> Matthew 8:3

> He touched her hand and the fever left her.
>
> Matthew 8:15

> After the crowd had been put outside, he went in and took the girl by the hand, and she got up.
>
> Matthew 9:25

> Then he touched their eyes and said, "According to your faith will it be done to you"; and their sight was restored.
>
> Matthew 9:29–30

> Jesus had compassion on them and touched their eyes. Immediately they received their sight and followed him.
>
> Matthew 20:34

> He took her by the hand and said to her, "*Talitha koum*!" (which means, "Little girl, I say to you, get up!"). Immediately the girl stood up and walked around (she was twelve years old).
>
> Mark 5:41–42

> Jesus took him by the hand and lifted him to his feet, and he stood up.
>
> Mark 9:27

These signs will accompany those who believe: . . . they will place their hands on sick people, and they will get well.

Mark 16:17–18

When the sun was setting, the people brought to Jesus all who had various kinds of sickness, and laying his hands on each one, he healed them.

Luke 4:40

Then he went up and touched the coffin, and those carrying it stood still. He said, "Young man, I say to you, get up!" The dead man sat up and began to talk, and Jesus gave him back to his mother.

Luke 7:14–15

He put his hands on her, and immediately she straightened up and praised God.

Luke 13:13

Taking him by the right hand, he helped him up, and instantly the man's feet and ankles became strong.

Acts 3:7

Placing his hands on Saul, he said, "Brother Saul, the Lord—Jesus, who appeared to you on the road as you were coming here—has sent me so that you may see again and be filled with the Holy Spirit." Immediately, something like scales fell from Saul's eyes, and he could see again.

Acts 9:17–18

He took her by the hand and helped her to her feet. Then he called the believers and the widows and presented her to them alive.

Acts 9:41

Paul went down, threw himself on the young man and put his arms around him. "Don't be alarmed," he said. "He's alive!"

Acts 20:10

Paul went in to see him and, after prayer, placed his hands on him and healed him.

Acts 28:8

Touch was so integral to the process of healing that people desiring healing sought to touch or be touched:

People brought all their sick to him and begged him to let the sick just touch the edge of his cloak, and all who touched him were healed.

Matthew 14:35–36

He had healed many, so that those with diseases were pushing forward to touch him.

Mark 3:10

One of the synagogue rulers, named Jairus, came there. Seeing Jesus, he fell at his feet and pleaded earnestly with him, "My little daughter is dying. Please come and put your hands on her so that she will be healed and live."

Mark 5:22–23

When she heard about Jesus, she came up behind him in the crowd and touched his cloak, because she thought, "If I just touch his clothes, I will be healed."

Mark 5:27–28

Everywhere he went—into villages, towns or countryside—they placed the sick in the marketplaces. They begged him to let them touch even the edge of his cloak, and all who touched him were healed.

Mark 6:56

Some people brought a man to him who was deaf and could hardly talk, and they begged him to place his hand on the man.

Mark 7:32

They came to Bethsaida, and some people brought a blind man and begged Jesus to touch him.

Mark 8:22

The people all tried to touch him, because power was coming from him and healing them all.

Luke 6:19

Prayers of Command

Not only did Christ and the apostles perform physical actions with their prayers, but they commanded others to action. Some believers today refer to these orders as "prayers of command" because, even though the Father is not being addressed, as He is in a regular prayer, the commands are being offered as an act of faith and part of the prayer process. It is helpful to see these prayers of command as an aspect of action prayers in which the action is not to be *performed* by the person praying but *commanded* by him or her.

Commonly in the New Testament the actions were commanded of the persons being healed. Among these commands are:

Get up. (Matthew 9:6; Luke 7:14; Acts 9:34)

Stand up on your feet! (Acts 14:10)

Come out! (John 11:43)

Walk. (Acts 3:6)

Stretch out your hand. (Matthew 12:13; Mark 3:5)

Be clean! (Matthew 8:3; Mark 1:41)

Go. (Mark 10:52)

Commands were also given to evil spirits:

Go! (Matthew 8:32)

Be quiet! Come out of him! (Mark 1:25; Luke 4:35)

In the name of Jesus Christ I command you to come out of her! (Acts 16:18)

In two instances we are not given the verbatim command with which Jesus rebuked the spirits before they departed (Matthew 17:18; Luke 4:41).

Jesus gave commands not only to sick persons and demons but even to the elements: "He got up, rebuked the wind and said to the waves, 'Quiet! Be still!'" (Mark 4:39; see Matthew 8:26).

"Secondhand" Touch

Two other instances are related to action prayers since touch is an element in them: Peter's shadow, which was believed to bring healing to those on whom it fell (Acts 5:15); and the handkerchiefs and aprons that had touched Paul and "were taken to the sick, and their illnesses were cured and the evil spirits left them" (Acts 19:12).

The matter of "secondhand" touch has been subject to much abuse. Radio and TV evangelists have traded, in exchange for an offering of at least a certain amount of money, "holy" handkerchiefs or "anointed" cloths that they have touched and allegedly infused with healing powers.

But Scripture is clear that we are not to take money in return for healing or offer to heal in exchange for a financial contribution. Gehazi suffered terribly for accepting money that Naaman gave in appreciation for his healing by Elisha (2 Kings 5:19–27) and Simon the Sorcerer received a strong rebuke from Peter for attempting to pay for and profit from spiritual power (Acts 8:18–24).

Uses of Action Prayers

Now that we have seen how action prayers are used in the New Testament in healing evangelism, we need to see why we should use them in our healing evangelism today. There are at least five reasons.

First, *action prayers are most often "gesture prayers" requesting healing from God.* Anointing a person with oil is asking for the anointing of the healing power of the Spirit. Touching is asking the Lord to touch the person. And so on. These are ways of begging God for mercy for the person needing healing.

The second reason to use action prayers is that *action prayers are seen not only by the Lord but by the person needing healing and by others present.* They build faith and hope in those who see them; and faith (as we have already seen) is an important element in healing.

Third, *action prayers are acts of obedience that express the faith of the one doing them.* Why do I lay hands on the sick? Because I am acting in obedience to Scripture and in the faith that God will honor my obedience. Somehow it will make a difference because I have obeyed Scripture and laid hands on this person.

I know what it is to lay hands on more than a hundred persons, one after the other. It takes time. After a while it becomes routine. Sometimes I feel power flowing through me and leaving me. Sometimes I feel nothing but tedium. Often I feel foolish and ask myself, *Why am I doing this?* Then I remind myself that I am obeying Scripture and believe, whether I feel it at the moment or not, that it will make a difference.

Later, when I invite those who have received a healing touch from Jesus to testify, they speak of having felt heat or power flowing through their bodies when I touched them. They speak of fever leaving, pain going, lame limbs getting new strength, eyesight improving. And most of them tie the instant of healing to the moment of my touch.

These times of healing prayer usually follow the sermon and Gospel invitation. Many of those healed have just received Christ. Some may have come for the healing prayer and obtained salvation while they waited.

As I listen to these testimonies, I realize that the Lord uses my touch for healing, even though He is perfectly capable of healing if I only pray and do not touch. I can also tell from the testimonies that these persons were strengthened in faith to believe that Jesus would touch them by the simple fact that I was touching them in His name. Faith, as well as my touch, was an element in their healing.

The fourth reason to use action prayers is that *touch communicates love and compassion.* Many people need that concrete expression of love. In purely psychological terms, the touch can be therapeutic. I read a study of the reasons people in Africa prefer traditional doctors (witch doctors) to medical doctors. One major reason: They find medical doctors cold, detached, impersonal. The witch doctors touch them, and Africans want that personal touch.

And finally, *action prayers are requests not only that the Lord anoint or touch these persons, but that a certain means be used.*

I am praying not only that Christ will touch them, but that He will touch them through my touch in His name; not only that He will anoint them with the Holy Spirit, but that He will anoint them with the Spirit even as I anoint them with oil. In this way the action becomes both the prayer and the means by which the prayer is answered.

Action prayers in which the lame are commanded to get up become the means by which the Lord gives faith to the lame, as well as the strength to rise. Commands to evil spirits to go are acts of authority over the spirits—the very authority Jesus gave us (Luke 10:19)—and are the means that force them to obey and go.

By praying action prayers we provide the Lord the means that He may well use in bringing about the desired healing or deliverance.

How Do Action Prayers Work?

When I was ministering in India in the autumn of 1993 under the auspices of the India Pentecostal Church, I was encouraged in almost every service, whether in a church or crusade, to pray for the sick. This gave me an opportunity to teach on healing and offer a model of healing prayer that would be balanced and scriptural.

After each sermon, while I was careful to make no unscriptural promises of healing, I invited those who wanted prayer to come forward. I prayed that the power of the Lord would be present to heal the sick (Luke 5:17; see also Luke 6:19). Then, following the example of Acts 28:8, I laid hands on each person, pointing out that my touch alone was of no value but that I was laying on hands in the name of Jesus and praying that He would touch every man, woman or child.

At each service in which I did this, a number of persons testified to having received an immediate healing touch from Jesus. In most cases they said that a headache or some other pain had left them. Some testified of improved eyesight. A few demonstrated that they could move limbs they had not been able to move. One man who had been partly paralyzed on one side by an accident could now raise his arm. Another man spoke of having had constant, severe back pain for more than thirty years, which ceased completely when I was praying.

Those who were not yet healed I urged not to be discouraged but to continue praying and trusting Jesus. "Your healing will come in His time," I said, "and according to His will."

When I use action prayers in Uganda, by contrast, where we have much larger crowds, it is difficult for me to touch everyone. In 1993 I brought a team with me from the States to help pray and to demonstrate to Ugandans how to set up prayer stations so that everyone can be prayed for personally.

At the close of each evangelistic rally I announced that everyone who needed it could receive prayer with the laying on of hands. I pointed to several locations around the area where a ministry team, usually consisting of one American and one or two Ugandans, was ready to pray with the laying on of hands. I urged everyone who was sick and all those tormented by evil spirits to go to one of the prayer stations.

Many in those rallies were prayed for.

Afterward a young schoolteacher on the team wrote a report for friends who had supported her trip and told them of the prayer ministry. "The Lord was so good to me," she said. "Everyone with demons went to Don or Peterson. I got to pray for headaches and stomachaches!"

We can understand this point of view. But if we are to do healing evangelism, we may encounter evil spirits and need to know what to do. That is the purpose of the following chapter.

12

When You Encounter Evil Spirits

"Lord, I pray for my friend Barbara. She is Your child. Fill her with Your Holy Spirit. Pour out Your Spirit on her and fill every inch of her being so completely that there will be no room for any spirit that is not of Jesus."

I had known Barbara (not her real name) for almost twenty years, since she and her husband had joined the church I then pastored. As I prayed for her now, my hand resting on her shoulder, suddenly her mouth opened and a voice that was not hers spoke to me through her lips:

"Leave us alone or we will destroy your ministry."

I recognized the ugly voice of the enemy. And in that split-second I thought back to an incident that had occurred during the days when I was first Barbara's pastor. She had called me because she had just taken massive amounts of sleeping pills and alcohol, was very sleepy and would die soon if someone did not come to her rescue. She had not wanted to do this, she added, but "voices" had commanded her to and she had been unable to refuse. I went to her house, gave her medicine to force her to vomit and stayed with her to keep her awake until her husband came home from work. It never occurred to me that the voices commanding Barbara were demonic.

Not recognizing the demonic was a typical mistake of my early ministry. My greatest regret is that for years I counseled people about problems I thought were psychological and never attempted deliverance. Indeed, I was convinced that a born-again person could not be bothered by evil spirits. Like many others, I believed that the Holy Spirit and an evil spirit cannot occupy the same body at the same time. Even with Barbara, though it is obvious to me today, it never occurred to me to attempt any kind of deliverance. I counseled with many people, especially ones with compulsive behavior or suicidal tendencies, who I now realize were likely the victims of spirits from which they needed deliverance. But I simply did not see it.

I will describe my deliverance ministry with Barbara later in this chapter. For now, let me simply recap that healing evangelism, as we have seen it in the New Testament, includes not only bringing wholeness to the sick but deliverance to the demonized. For years, sadly, misunderstanding kept me from the latter important ministry.

In this chapter I aim to set forth some of the things I have learned so that you, with me, can enter into the full ministry of healing evangelism.

Demonization

Our misunderstanding is due partly to the word *possessed*, a poor translation in the King James that, tragically, is carried over into many modern translations. The word suggests ownership, whereas a demon does not own a believer—or anybody else, for that matter.

The biblical word is literally *demonized* or *to have a demon*. A whole range of activity can be considered demonization.

At one end of the scale, all of us experience temptations and evil thoughts that are placed in our minds by demons. At the other end are the instances of severe demonization wrongly referred to as "possession." But even the severely demonized are not totally controlled. The Gadarene was infested with a legion of demons that manifested themselves in terrible behavior (Mark 5:3–5), but they could not prevent him from bringing them to the place they least wanted to be: at the feet of Jesus. "When he saw Jesus from a distance, he ran and fell on his knees in front of him" (verse 6).

How much control can demons exercise over the truly regenerate? Right after Peter confessed Christ by the power of the Father, Satan spoke through his mouth denying the coming death and resurrection of Christ (Matthew 16:16–23). Ananias and Sapphira were apparently believers and gave generously to the church. Nevertheless, they conspired to deceive the church about money they held back from the sale of some property. (We all know believers who might do such a thing today.) Peter indicated that they lied because "Satan has so filled your heart" (Acts 5:3).

Many pastors have known Christians who gave evidence of demonization. When these pastors challenged the spirits, as I finally did in Barbara's case (almost twenty years after the episode with the pills), the demons manifested themselves by speaking back. If regenerate persons cannot be demonized, how is it that some of them curse their pastors in voices not their own?

The view that believers cannot be demonized is a consequence of the theory that all gifts of the Holy Spirit have ceased. If God does not perform miracles today, then He does not cast out demons today. And if He does not cast out demons today, then either there are no demons to cast out, or else Satan is more powerful than God since he can afflict people with demons and God can do nothing about it. Such reasoning leads to the conclusion that Christ drove out all demons during His incarnation.

Nowhere does Scripture indicate that demonic activity would diminish after the time of Christ. On the contrary, it predicts an increase in the last days. The Bible views the whole period from the first to the second comings of Christ as the last days (1 John 2:18). The demonic influences that characterize this age will grow increasingly intense as the age draws to a close (2 Thessalonians 2:9; 1 Timothy 4:1). And as we are led to expect the intensification of demonic influence at this time, so we may anticipate the increase of the gifts and power of the Holy Spirit to counteract these evil forces.

The Problem of Garbage

The Holy Spirit indwells the spirit of each regenerate person—the spirit where evil spirits are never again able to enter. It is obvious, however, that spirits may attach themselves to the bodies of believers when they have opportunity. Some believers have demons they inherited from their ancestors. Others have them as a result of drug abuse, occult involvement or some other sin before their conversion. Many were victims of child abuse, especially sexual abuse. (This was Barbara's situation.)

These demons left the human spirit at the time of regeneration but continued to remain attached to the person. They might have been driven out when the person was converted but they were not.

Some believers have acquired demons as a result of sin after conversion, during a period of backsliding, although this is more rare.

Whatever the situation, whenever the infestation, Charles H. Kraft (professor at the School of World Mission, Fuller Theological Seminary) points out that a problem with demons is like a problem with rats. Rats are drawn to garbage. If you get rid of your rats but do nothing about the garbage, the rats will soon come back. Demons attach themselves to people with garbage in their lives. These people usually need emotional healing from bitterness, hatred, unforgiveness or something else. If the demons are driven from them but the basic problems are not healed, the demons will, as Jesus taught (Matthew 12:43–45), soon be back.

Kraft prefers to deal with the garbage first. He counsels and prays with his clients about attitudes that need healing. As these problems become resolved, the demons that have attached themselves to the problems become weaker and easier to handle and can soon be run off without difficulty. But Kraft recognizes it is also valid to deal first with the demons and then enter into a program of counseling to deal with the inner needs. (See his book *Defeating Dark Angels: Breaking Demonic Oppression in the Believer's Life*, Servant, 1992).

I often encounter situations in which I am able to deliver a demonized person but have no opportunity to counsel with him or her in the future. This is especially true when I am the visiting minister in a church. So I try whenever possible to refer such a person to someone for counseling.

There is a difference between demonization and mental illness, but the two may be related. If a demonized person is also mentally ill, he or she needs to receive deliverance and also to be referred to a Christian psychiatrist.

No Big Deal!

We talked in chapter 2 about Jesus' response to the exuberant comment of the 72 who said, "Lord, even the demons submit to us in your name" (Luke 10:17):

> I saw Satan fall like lightning from heaven. I have given you authority to trample on snakes and scorpions and to

> overcome all the power of the enemy; nothing will harm you. However, do not rejoice that the spirits submit to you, but rejoice that your names are written in heaven.
>
> verses 18–20

I said that I see a direct correlation between Satan falling from heaven and the successful ministry of the 72 that had just been completed. So in terms of deliverance ministry today, I would paraphrase Jesus' remark in this way:

> You are amazed that the demons submit to you? That's no big deal! Of course they submit to you. They're weak and puny. I am defeating them and giving you power over them. You have power to trample on them—those evil snakes and scorpions. In fact, you have power to overcome all the power of Satan. Don't be afraid of their threats. They can't hurt you. So don't rejoice over something so trivial as the submission of those little scorpions. If you want to rejoice, rejoice over something really significant: that your names are included among the saved in the Lamb's Book of Life!

Demons rule by fear. By their tricks they terrorize people in Africa and many other lands. But they are more afraid of you, if you are a believer in Christ, than you can ever be of them. You represent the authority of Jesus to them. You have the power to cast them out and destroy their works. They know, even if you forget, that "you, dear children, are from God and have overcome them, because the one who is in you is greater than the one who is in the world" (1 John 4:4).

So do not let them bluff you. Never let them frighten you, because that just plays into their hands. Let them know you are aware of the tremendous authority of Jesus over them and that you know you wield that authority by the indwelling Spirit.

Driving out evil spirits is not a gift of the Spirit. Discerning them is—a gift we need to recognize that they are there and know how to speak to them. But the power to drive them out belongs to every believer (Mark 16:17). It is not reserved for certain anointed evangelists or specially gifted saints.

Evil spirits know *you* have that power. Act and speak in that confidence.

Deliverance

The first thing to do when you are in the presence of a person you suspect may be demonized is to pray silently to bind the demons in the name of Jesus (Matthew 16:19). Forbid them from doing any harm to their victim or causing any violence. Forbid them from overhearing your conversation with the victim, especially any plans or appointments you might make. Forbid them from causing the victim to thrash about, vomit or do anything to harm himself or you. Take authority over the situation in the name of Jesus.

Also be sure to pray earnestly for the power of the Holy Spirit. Invite Him to come in power and take control. Yield the situation to Him and tell Him He is free to do what He wishes. Ask Him for wisdom, discernment and direction in all you say and do. And throughout the session, keep on calling Him for more and more power.

A team approach is valuable. If you suspect you may be facing the need for deliverance and you are alone with the person, you may wish to make an appointment for later when one or more team members can join you. A small prayer team is helpful because their prayers together with yours will have more power than yours alone. Also, they may receive insights that you do not about what to ask and how to pray. If you are assisting a person of the opposite sex, it is important to have a person of that same sex present to protect you against false accusations of sexual misconduct.

Be careful, however, to invite only persons sympathetic to what you are doing. You do not want curious spectators from whose skepticism the demons may draw power. Remember how, in the biblical resuscitation accounts we looked at, the person praying sent all or most of the onlookers out of the room.

Never attempt deliverance in a public or large group setting. Respect the privacy of the person you are trying to help. Take him or her and your small prayer team aside to a small room for personal ministry.

You may ask the person, "The symptoms you describe are sometimes associated with evil spirits. Do you think there is any possibility that evil spirits may be part of your problem?"

Often he or she will answer, "Yes, of course, that's precisely my problem. I have known it for years. They often speak to me in my mind and tell me to do terrible things. I'm relieved that you asked. I wanted to tell you but I was afraid you wouldn't believe me, that you might think I was crazy for believing in evil spirits."

Whether or not the person immediately admits the problem of demons, try to explore, as part of your counseling, what kind of "garbage" is in his or her life. Have he or his parents or any family members ever been involved in occult activities? What about ouija boards? Tarot cards? Astrology? Fortunetellers? Freemasonry or other occult organizations? New Age literature? Hypnotism? As you develop your relationship with this person, try to find out if he or she harbors bitterness, unforgiveness or hatred toward anyone, or if he or she was ever abused as a child.

Eventually all this garbage must be repented of and renounced. Forgiveness must be obtained from the Lord. Since the demons gain ground for victimizing people in these ways, removing the demons requires removing the things to which demons attach themselves.

As you explore the possible ground that the demons hold, pray to the Holy Spirit for discernment. He may suggest to you things you should inquire about.

After you have learned as much as you can, pray. Don't be afraid to place your hand on the person as you do so. The personal contact is helpful to him or her and aggravating to the spirits.

Exactly what you will pray depends on what the person told you and what he or she understands. If he or she denies the possibility that demons are present, you can pray a prayer similar to the one in the opening paragraph of this chapter. No one is offended or frightened if you pray that he or she will be filled completely with the Holy Spirit.

You may ask the person, "Since these symptoms are sometimes associated with demonic activity, and we can't rule out that possibility, do you mind if I pray that if there are any spirits present that are not of Jesus, they will go and go quietly?" Few will object to such a proposal.

You may command any spirits present to "go and go quietly" with no manifestation. On the other hand, you do not know for sure that there are demons present unless they manifest themselves. If they manifest, you may get information from them regarding the "ground" they occupy that will be helpful in ejecting them.

Praying a prayer like the one in the opening paragraph may force them out of hiding and compel them to manifest themselves, just as happened with Barbara. You may find it necessary, however, to command them in the name of Jesus to come out of hiding and manifest themselves to you. Be sure to include the command that they do the victim no harm in the process.

Once they begin speaking, command them to tell the truth and tell you their names, under what conditions they were able to enter this person and what their ground is presently for being there. Their names are often clues to the kind of trouble they cause and the kind of garbage to which they attach themselves. When you command them to tell the truth, they may not tell it immediately. Do not trust any information they give you; but on the other hand, with the Holy Spirit to give you discernment, you may get some information that will be useful in deliverance or counseling.

Do not allow them to put on a show for you. Do not allow them to try to frighten you or bargain with you. Do not feel it necessary to bring up the spirits one by one and hold lengthy conversations with them all. Get the name of the leading spirit and deal with all of them, if possible, through it.

When the evil spirits have manifested themselves, when you have learned about the ground of their presence and when the person has repented of the sins to which the demons have attached themselves, then it is time to command them to go in the name of Jesus. It is usually best *not* to send them out one by one. Command them all to go at once—while doing no harm to the victim and without causing him or her to vomit—to wherever Jesus sends them. Forbid them from "splitting" (leaving early or going partially into another person so they can return later).

When you command them to go, they are not likely to go immediately. You may have to repeat this command many times. They will try to argue with you, but do not let them. Keep pleading the name of Jesus and the power of His blood. Let there be an atmosphere of praise in the room. Members of your team might sing praise songs and read Scriptures of praise. Praising God increases the presence of the power of the Spirit. Prayer in tongues as well as English also increases the effectiveness of deliverance.

After the spirits go, you will want to rejoice with the former victim, offer counsel on further steps he or she should take and make arrangements for follow-up counseling with yourself or someone else. (A discussion of counseling prayer follows in chapter 13.)

Barbara

Almost twenty years after the demons caused Barbara to take an overdose of pills, I confronted them in the situation I described at the beginning of this chapter. We got rid of a number of minor spirits easily, but one powerful leader was difficult to dislodge. I urged Barbara to pray and confess to the Lord the sins we knew were giving the spirits ground.

"I can't," she said. "There's too much resistance. They won't let me."

I urged her to pray, confess to the Lord Jesus that He was the Lord in her life and acknowledge many other truths about His Person and work. Again she said she could not because of demonic resistance.

I confronted the lead demon and demanded that he tell me his name.

"That's not for you to know," he said defiantly through Barbara's mouth.

I commanded again.

Barbara's mouth was clenched tight. No sound or name came forth.

I prayed for discernment from the Holy Spirit. Then I said, "That's all right. I know your name anyway. It's Suicide, isn't it? Suicide, in the name of the Lord Jesus Christ, I command you and all those with you to leave now and go where Jesus sends you. I command you to go and go quietly."

Suddenly Barbara, who had been looking understandably tense all evening, leaned forward in her chair and relaxed. Her mouth opened and her own voice poured forth the most magnificent extemporaneous prayer I have ever heard. Anointed by the Holy Spirit, she confessed and renounced all the sins she had been unable to confess. Her acknowledgment of the Lordship of Jesus Christ over her life was a hymn of heartfelt praise.

The day after her deliverance she asked me, "Do you think all the spirits left last night?"

"If there were any hanging around," I answered, "their presence was totally nullified. They had no power at all. They were unable to prevent you from praying the prayer that they most wanted you not to pray."

Barbara nodded, smiling. She was free.

I only wished I had known to do this years before.

13

Not All Hurt Is Physical

Many who have hurts need prayer, but not for physical healing. Their hurts are emotional. Many others have physical problems that are to some extent the result of psychological problems. Anger, bitterness, unforgiveness and low self-esteem are among the kinds of emotional baggage they carry. These hurts are the very kinds of garbage to which demons sometimes attach themselves, as we saw in the last chapter. We who have ministries of healing evangelism—and this should include every Christian—need to consider ways of helping those with such needs, either as part of the deliverance process, as follow-up for those who are delivered or as help for those who are hurting but need no deliverance.

These problems are dealt with not by prayer alone but by a combination of prayer and counseling. *Prayer counseling* is a phrase that is sometimes used of this kind of ministry, either to define a particular method or, more generically, to describe all combinations of prayer and counseling for the purpose of emotional healing. I use the term *counseling prayer* to avoid confusion with a particular methodology and to emphasize that this is still basically a ministry of prayer. I counsel as I engage in healing prayer rather than simply pray while I am counseling.

In prayer times during evangelistic crusades or at the conclusion of church services, counseling prayer can be offered only on a limited basis. Nevertheless, even a crusade evangelist has opportunities to make appointments to engage in counseling prayer, and pastors and lay Christians have ample opportunity to do counseling prayer in connection with the ministry of the local church.

Areas of Controversy

In recent years the ministry of what is variously called emotional healing, inner healing or the healing of memories has been the subject of much controversy. Christians who teach in this area borrow insights from secular psychologists who, they believe, have been allowed by the common grace of God to discover some aspects of God's truth. But a few Christians oppose any use of psychology, even the use of current terminology and categories.

It goes without saying that any insight from secular psychology needs to be measured against the teaching of the Word of God and be consistent with it in all respects.

Let's look in particular at two issues related to inner healing that have been misunderstood.

Self-Esteem

The first issue is the concept of self-image or self-esteem. This concept, basic to counseling prayer, is considered by some to be a category of secular psychology contrary to the Word of God. They argue that we are to be humble, recognize that we are sinners and not to "think of yourself more highly than you ought" (Romans 12:3). To those who argue this way, the Bible is commanding us to have low self-esteem while secularists are encouraging high self-esteem.

Let's leave this objection aside for a minute and see how the argument of secular psychologists develops.

They say that a person's self-image affects his or her behavior. If he has little respect for himself, he will behave in ways that may harm him. He may, for instance, abuse drugs and alcohol. If he thinks of himself as little better than an animal, he will behave little better than an animal. (Thus, you hear even non-Christians comment that some people have "the morals of an alley cat.") On the other hand, say these secular psychologists, if a person sees himself as having worth and dignity, he will behave as a person of worth and dignity. Thus, an important way of improving a person's behavior is improving his sense of self-worth.

Christians who object to this line of thinking and resist the notion of self-worth overlook the fact that most scriptural teaching on holiness is also based on positive teaching on self-worth, though it may not be framed in those words. Throughout Scripture we are exhorted to derive our self-image from our relationship with God and behave accordingly.

The Israelites were told that, as God's chosen nation, they were to behave as the people of a holy God. "Be holy, because I am holy," God said to them (Leviticus 11:44–45; 19:2; 20:7–8). The New Testament repeats this admonition (1 Peter 1:16).

Most of Paul's letters are divided into two sections. The first section is doctrinal and explains our privileges as the redeemed children of God. The second section is practical and tells us how to live in the light of the fact that we are the redeemed children of God. The first three chapters of

Ephesians tell us about the high calling we received when God chose and predestined us before the foundation of the world, and Ephesians 4–6 tell us to "live a life worthy of the calling you have received" (4:1).

Self-esteem is not, therefore, an ungodly concept that Christians have borrowed from humanists, but a scriptural concept that humanists have borrowed from Christianity, even if they have not always done so consciously.

The Use of Imagination

The second issue in which inner healing is controversial is in the therapeutic value of an active imagination. Let me give an example.

A woman has memories of being abused by her father—memories that have caused many present spiritual problems, including anger and unforgiveness. Her memories are a cause of her low self-esteem, since she reasons like this: "As a child I was treated as an object of sexual satisfaction by my father. So I'm not a worthwhile person to be treated with dignity and respect, but only a worthless object to be abused."

Some Christian counselors will try to heal this hurtful memory by asking this woman to use her imagination to "reconstruct" the memory.

"What was Jesus doing at the time?" they might ask her. "Was He grieving at what your father was doing? Was Jesus providing protection so that you would not be abused worse than you were? Was Jesus trying to bring your father to repentance? Use your imagination to reconstruct this event with Jesus in it. And from now on, whenever you remember this incident, use the new, reconstructed, Christ-centered memory."

Some object to this kind of counseling, saying that it uses "visualization," a technique borrowed from New Age thinking. They further argue that the Bible speaks of imagination only as something evil, as in these verses:

> The LORD saw how great man's wickedness on the earth had become, and that every inclination [*imagination,* KJV] of the thoughts of his heart was only evil all the time.
>
> Genesis 6:5

> We demolish arguments [*imaginations,* KJV] and every pretension that sets itself up against the knowledge of God.
>
> 2 Corinthians 10:5

That the Bible teaches that imagination can be evil and set against God does not deny that imagination can be used for good purposes. We can use our God-given gift of active imagination for good *or* evil. Indeed, the verse from Corinthians above goes on to say, "And we take captive every thought to make it obedient to Christ." Thus, we are to change our thinking so that instead of imagining evil things, we imagine good things and make our imaginations "obedient to Christ."

Many Scriptures urge us to bring our imaginations under the Lordship of Christ so that our thoughts are centered on Him. For example:

> If my people, who are called by my name, will . . . seek my face. . . .
>
> 2 Chronicles 7:14

> I have set the LORD always before me.
>
> Psalm 16:8

> I saw the Lord always before me.
>
> Acts 2:25

We fix our eyes not on what is seen, but on what is unseen.

2 Corinthians 4:18

Finally, brothers, whatever is true, whatever is noble, whatever is right, whatever is pure, whatever is lovely, whatever is admirable—if anything is excellent or praiseworthy—think about such things.

Philippians 4:8

Set your minds on things above, not on earthly things.

Colossians 3:2

Let us fix our eyes on Jesus.

Hebrews 12:2

Proponents of the New Age teach that every person has divine power to change reality. Use your mind to "visualize" a different reality, they say, and you will create a new reality by mind power.

This is very different from what the Bible teaches when it tells you to see the Lord always before you, to seek His face and to fix your eyes on Jesus. When a person is counseled to reconstruct a memory by seeing Jesus in the incident, he or she is being counseled to follow Scriptures like the ones we just looked at. Such counsel is clearly counter to the teaching of the New Age movement.

Healing Prayer with Counseling

In counseling prayer we deal with problems not by prayer alone, as I said at the beginning of this chapter, but by a combination of prayer and counseling. Let me offer some insights into a few common problems, and then some guidelines from my own ministry.

Insights

We have mentioned several times that many Christians are crippled spiritually because of anger, bitterness and unforgiveness. Such attitudes are sin, but they can be caused by memories of mistreatment in the past. In order to be rid of these sins, a person needs to be delivered from the harmful power of these memories.

Other Christians are hampered in their spiritual growth by low self-esteem. Because they do not see their own worth, it is difficult for them to see their worth in the eyes of God or even believe that God loves them. They are improperly motivated to live according to their high calling in Christ because they find it difficult to believe that God has really called to Himself persons as "worthless" as they are. It is hard for them to conceive of themselves as creatures made in the image of God, much less as redeemed children of God who bear the family likeness and are to live according to the values of the divine family.

Their low self-esteem may be the result of having been treated as worthless in the past by parents or others who were important to them. Because those they valued did not value them, they cannot value themselves. Their memories of how they were treated must be dealt with before their hurt can be healed and they can be lifted up to see themselves scripturally.

Many memories exist in the subconscious mind but are blotted out of the conscious mind. This is particularly true of many who were abused sexually as children. They feel the hurt and anger daily but do not consciously remember the abuse and do not know why they are hurting.

Much compulsive behavior is caused by such hurts. Abuse of drugs, alcohol, sex, food, gambling, shopping and other behaviors gives a momentary high that helps to cover the inner hurt. People often do not know why they have these compulsions because they do not understand why they are hurting. They may seek recovery from a certain addiction and fall quickly into another. The recovering alcoholic, for example, may become a compulsive gambler. The problem was not the particular activity but the fact that the compulsion is due to an inner hurt and shame. Only when the hurt and shame are healed will he or she be delivered from compulsivity.

Guidelines

Great sensitivity is needed when you are praying with people for emotional healing. Be sensitive to the individual to perceive how he or she is hurting. Be sensitive, too, to the Holy Spirit for the insights He will give you into the person's needs.

It is usually not enough simply to pray that a person be delivered from anger or a particular compulsion. You need to take time (often several sessions are necessary) and ask questions to help bring out the root problem. The person may need time to go back through his memory bank to discover for himself the things that are causing his hurt.

Once the most basic memories and hurts are revealed, either by the individual or by impressions from the Holy Spirit that the individual confirms, then the real work begins. The individual must be brought to forgive those who hurt him and reconstruct his memory so that the compassionate role of Jesus is understood in otherwise painful incidents.

Only the Holy Spirit can replace anger with forgiveness, and hatred with love. Only the Holy Spirit can enable a person to see the redeeming love of Jesus in the painful incidents of the past. Only the Holy Spirit can heal the pain of inner hurts and replace it with peace and joy. Counseling prayer is, therefore, a spiritual more than a psychological ministry. Counseling may be necessary to detect the problem but prayer is needed to heal it.

Since demons sometimes attach themselves to these hurts, and since demons cause bitterness, unforgiveness and compulsion, counseling prayer should include deliverance prayer that any spirits not of Jesus be removed and that the person be filled with the Holy Spirit and the love of God.

Sometimes the greatest therapy for a hurting person is to feel you, a loving Christian brother or sister, laying a hand on him and praying with compassion that his anger be taken away, that his pain be replaced with peace and joy, that his bitterness be replaced with forgiveness and that he be enabled to see himself as God sees him—as a special child for whom God has a glorious plan of holiness and glory in Christ.

Part 5

Healing Evangelism in Different Settings

Healing evangelism can take place at a private bedside, at a home meeting, at a church service or in a mass crusade. Here are practical suggestions for all of these situations.

14

Sickbed Evangelism

When we think of healing evangelism, many of us think of large meetings. But healing evangelism can be done in other contexts as well—and sometimes more effectively.

I was in the Bombay Airport talking with K. P. Yohannan, founder and director of Gospel for Asia, an excellent mission that provides support for indigenous evangelists who are preaching and doing church-planting within their own countries. We were discussing unreached villages that have no Christian witness and that are often hostile to the Gospel when it is first presented.

"How do workers with Gospel for Asia evangelize these villages?" I asked.

"Once our evangelists move into villages like that," he replied, "we advise them to do nothing but fast and pray for one week. Then we advise them to seek out severely demonized people—because of paganism, there are many such persons in these villages—and cast out their demons. This is to be done quietly, not in public ministry."

Word gets quickly around the village, K. P. continued, that these people have been set free by the name of Jesus. This produces an openness and interest on the part of the villagers that provides opportunities for public ministry.

Biblical Precedents

There are many biblical precedents for private ministry. A number of sick people healed in the New Testament were healed in private settings. Among them:

- Peter's mother-in-law (Matthew 8:14–15; Mark 1:30–31; Luke 4:38–39)
- Jairus' daughter (Matthew 9:18–26; Mark 5:22–43; Luke 8:41–56)
- Aeneas (Acts 9:33–34)
- Dorcas (Acts 9:36–41)
- Publius (Acts 28:7–8)

These were all sickbed (or deathbed) scenes in which the evangelist went to the person to be healed. Although the healings were done privately, word spread so that there was a public evangelistic effect (Matthew 9:26; Acts 9:35, 42; 28:9).

The movie *Shadowlands*, which tells the love story of C. S. ("Jack") Lewis and Joy Gresham, indicates that right after their marriage Joy's cancer went into a brief remission that allowed them to take a short trip to Golden Valley. (Actually, Joy's remission lasted six months and allowed trips to Ireland and Greece.)

Hollywood does not tell us the reason for the remission: the healing ministry of the Rev. Peter Bide, an Anglican clergyman and a former pupil of Lewis'.

"Jack had heard that Bide was a healer," writes George Sayer in *Jack*, his biography of Lewis (Crossway, 1994). "He asked him to come and lay his hands on Joy and pray for her recovery."

When Bide arrived they invited him to conduct their private wedding ceremony.

"Bide agreed," Sayer writes, "and said he would perform the ceremony the day after he had laid his hands on her and prayed for her recovery." A friend of Bide's told me that he also anointed her with oil. And it was after this that Joy went into remission.

I understand why Hollywood omitted this important detail from a film marketed to a general audience. But it gives Christians the opportunity to tell the real story behind the film and turn healing into an opportunity for evangelism.

Another biblical reinforcement for private prayers for healing is found in James. He said the elders of the Church should visit the sick and pray for them with the anointing of oil (5:14–15). Sickbed healings were expected to become a regular part of the ongoing ministry of the Church, although James focused more on the pastoral healing of Christians who send for the elders than on healing evangelism.

Other healings in the New Testament took place publicly but not in the presence of a crowd, so they were more like private healings:

- The lame man at the pool of Bethesda (John 5:1–15)
- A blind man (John 9:1–7)
- Lazarus (John 11:1–44)
- The Gadarene demoniac (Matthew 8:28–34; Mark 5:1–20; Luke 8:26–39)

In other instances, people who were met in public were taken aside for a private healing. Jesus did this with a deaf man (Mark 7:33) and a blind man (Mark 8:23).

Advantages of Private Ministry

When healing evangelism is not limited to public crusades but ministered in private, there are several obvious advantages.

First, some persons can be ministered to only if we visit them on their sickbeds.

Second, the person praying has the opportunity to control the atmosphere. He or she can determine who is and is not present in the sickroom at the time of the prayer. We saw in chapter 6 that Elijah, Elisha, Jesus and Peter all put people out of the room or took the sick person to a private room. In this way, as we have seen, you can be assured that only persons of faith are present and that the power of the Holy Spirit will not be drained by the presence of unbelief.

A third advantage to private sessions for healing is that they allow more time for prayer and healing to take place. Sometimes healings occur gradually over minutes and even hours as prayer ministry continues for the person. A public situation does not offer the same opportunity for extended prayer and ministry for one individual.

Some years ago I was holding services in a Presbyterian church in New Mexico. A woman in the congregation asked the elders to come to her home and pray for her healing according to James 5:14. This was done frequently in that church. The pastor invited me, as a visiting elder, to take part in the ministry.

Gathered in the living room were the woman and her husband, the church elders, the pastor and I. The woman explained that they had been trying for a long time to have a child, but that she had never conceived. Some medical problem, she believed, was preventing conception, which is what she was requesting healing for.

The pastor read the passage in James 5, including verse 16: "Confess your sins to each other and pray for each other so that you may be healed. The prayer of a righteous man is powerful and effective." He pointed out that Scripture links healing with prayer but also with confession of sins, which are a barrier to wholeness and health. Then, beginning with himself and continuing with the elders, the pastor had us go around the circle in the living room, each confessing a sin.

Finally we came to the husband and wife. They confessed that there were serious problems in their relationship, which they feared were contributing to their inability to conceive. That night, in the presence of the elders, they confessed sins to one another and forgave one another. Then we anointed them with oil and prayed that the wife would soon conceive.

A short time afterward she did conceive, and later gave birth to a healthy child.

Private prayer sessions are not the only place to do healing evangelism, of course. In the next chapter we will discuss healing evangelism in larger, semi-private settings.

15

A Hole in the Roof

We are all familiar with the story of the men who broke a hole in the roof of a private home where Jesus was preaching in order to lower their friend to Jesus for healing (Matthew 9:1–8; Mark 2:1–12; Luke 5:17–26).

I used to speculate about the reaction of the owner of the home. Perhaps you have wondered about that, too. Now I suspect that the owner was understanding, for I believe it was Jesus' own house!

Early in His public ministry Jesus left Nazareth, where He had been reared, and "went and lived in Capernaum" (Matthew 4:13). The incident with the roof happened in "his own town" (Matthew 9:1), Capernaum, where His ministry was based.

We read in the same chapter in Matthew, "When he had gone indoors. . ." (9:28) and, "While they were going out. . ." (9:32). All this suggests to me that there was a particular house where Jesus usually stayed. Perhaps He owned it, or perhaps a relative or friend owned it and allowed Him to call it home.

Mark wrote:

> A few days later, when Jesus again entered Capernaum, the people heard that he had come home. So many gathered that there was no room left, not even outside the door, and he preached the word to them.
>
> Mark 2:1

It was at this house, when the people of that town heard that "he had come home" and gathered to hear him preach, where the roof was opened.

We have often missed seeing this because we have tended to interpret the verse "The Son of Man has no place to lay his head" (Matthew 8:20) as meaning that Jesus had no permanent home and was transient. But in the light of the above evidence, we must reject that interpretation. He was more likely speaking of His lifestyle as an itinerant preacher, most often away from home, needing a host or sponsor in every village He visited—and sometimes finding none. When we accept this understanding of "no place to lay his head," then the information about His home in Capernaum becomes self-evident.

The point I am leading to is this: One of the places Jesus did healing evangelism was His own home. When He was home, crowds gathered there to hear Him preach and have Him heal their sick. It is an opportunity for healing evangelism that we can consider, too.

In the last chapter we spoke of healing prayer that takes place in private settings, often in people's homes. In this chapter we will focus on the opportunities available in semi-private group meetings in homes and similar settings.

Home Group Meetings

Normally when you hold a meeting in your home, whether it is a Bible study or prayer meeting or home fellowship gathering, you are in control of who comes and what the spiritual atmosphere will be. In the case of the man lowered through the roof, of course, so many people showed up that the meeting seems to have gotten out of hand! Still, a meeting in a home is generally a "semi-private" and not a public meeting.

You have less time to pray for individuals in such a meeting than you do when you are praying for someone privately. At the same time, with more people present, you have more of an opportunity for evangelism.

The home "cell group" meetings of the Yoido Full Gospel Church in Seoul, Korea, are an excellent example of healing evangelism taking place in a semi-private setting. The groups meet in homes and participation is limited to the regular members of the group and those they invite.

There are many small group home meetings among Christians in the U.S. Many of these are cell groups (or "growth groups") of particular congregations. Others are gatherings of like-minded believers from a cross-section of churches. Many of these home meetings are devoted primarily to Bible study. Some are specifically for prayer. In some, healing takes place as the members pray for one another. Few, however, are examples of healing evangelism. Most focus on the needs of the members of the group. Discipleship (which is important) is stressed while outreach and evangelism are often overlooked. In fact, there is a tendency for such groups to become introspective and ingrown, which makes evangelism and outreach unlikely.

Those of us concerned for healing evangelism should seek to initiate and develop home meetings devoted to evangelism. These could be on the Yoido model, but there are other models as well.

Other Settings

There are other locations besides homes where semi-private healing evangelism can take place.

Retreat centers provide good locations. My friends Bill and Delores Winder of Shreveport, Louisiana (you will read more about them in chapter 17), have an itinerant healing ministry that has acquired a small retreat center in nearby Jefferson, Texas. Their ministry, Fellowship Foundation, holds many weekend retreats at Shepherd's Pasture, which is typical of many retreat centers and where much healing evangelism takes place. Anyone in need of spiritual renewal or healing is free to come anytime and stay at Shepherd's Pasture for a personal retreat.

You do not need to own a retreat center, of course, to use such a facility. When the Winders are not holding their own retreats at Shepherd's Pasture, they rent it to other groups. The same is true with other centers.

On a larger scale is the Prayer Mountain of the Yoido Church in Seoul. On any given day (as I said in chapter 1) three thousand people are praying there, ten thousand on weekends. Some have come for a few hours, some for days or weeks. The day I was there I met a woman coming off a forty-day fast. There are many chapels where prayer meetings are conducted. Often several prayer meetings are going on simultaneously. There are also many "prayer grottos"—individual chambers for private prayer. There are no recreational facilities and no dining area, except a small room where one can get soup and rice only. Everyone has come to fast and pray.

Many churches in Korea have similar Prayer Mountains.

One international renewal organization, Presbyterian & Reformed Renewal Ministries International, conducts what it calls "Prayer Mountain Retreats" with a program patterned after the Prayer Mountains of Korea. They are weekend retreats for the purpose of prayer. PRRMI has no retreat center (it hopes to have one someday) but rents the facilities of other groups.

Sometimes PRRMI uses a church building with a motel nearby for retreats called "Prayer Mountains"—not "Prayer Retreats," because that name suggests a weekend conference with lots of teaching on prayer. There is little teaching at Prayer Mountains. The people have come to do the work of prayer. Considerable healing takes place at PRRMI's Prayer Mountains.

Another location for healing evangelism, similar to a retreat center, is a healing center. This idea is not new. In fact, I first learned from the writings of Andrew Murray about the founder of one of these centers more than a century ago.

Rev. Johann Christoph Blumhardt was a Lutheran pastor in Moettlingen in the Black Forest of Germany. A great revival broke out under his ministry. Many were converted and many healed. Beginning in 1844, many he prayed for received remarkable healings and deliverances. Many sick people came and stayed in his home while seeking healing.

The ministry soon outgrew his home. The Lord provided for Blumhardt to acquire a large mansion in nearby Bad Boll. It had 42 rooms that he was able to convert into sleeping apartments. Soon Bad Boll was filled with a community of people seeking healing. There were normally from 100 to 150 people resident at any one time.

A more modern example of a healing center is operated in Jacksonville, Florida, by Christian Healing Ministries of the Rev. Francis MacNutt. It is not a residential community but more of a spiritual outpatient clinic in a building that was formerly an Episcopal church. Retreats and services are held in a lovely sanctuary, and the rooms that had once been Sunday school classrooms are now offices and counseling rooms. The paid staff includes trained psychologists and counselors. One or two medical doctors participate on a part-time basis. There are also many volunteer intercessors who serve on prayer teams. People in need of healing come to the center for counseling and prayer. Medical healing and healing prayer are united in a marvelous holistic approach. (The address of Christian Healing Ministries, along with Fellowship Foundation, is listed in appendix 4 on p. 249.)

There are many possibilities, as I have tried to show, for a middle way between doing healing evangelism in private sickbed prayer sessions and, on the other hand, in large public church services and mass evangelistic crusades. Finding opportunities for healing evangelism in private or semi-private settings is not difficult; and developing the approaches that are best for you is the result of sanctified imagination plus sensitivity to the leading of the Holy Spirit.

What about doing healing evangelism in church services? What format would healing ministry follow in a traditional church? Are there ways *your* church can be encouraged to be open to a healing ministry, if it does not have one already? The following chapter offers suggestions.

16

Don't Fall Asleep before the Healing Service!

The New Testament does not give much information about how to do healing evangelism in church services. In fact, it describes only one church service in which a healing took place, and the healing was clearly unplanned:

> On the first day of the week we came together to break bread. Paul spoke to the people and, because he intended to leave the next day, kept on talking until midnight. There were many lamps in the upstairs room where we were meeting. Seated in a window was a young man named Eutychus, who was sinking into a deep sleep as Paul talked on and on. When he was sound asleep, he fell to the ground from the third story and was picked up dead. Paul went down, threw himself on the young man and put his arms around him. "Don't be alarmed," he said. "He's alive!" Then he went upstairs again and broke bread and ate. After

talking until daylight, he left. The people took the young man home alive and were greatly comforted.

Acts 20:7–12

Since in this chapter we are exploring the use of healing evangelism in churches, and since Christian church services were patterned after synagogue services, it is instructive to start by identifying from the New Testament any aspects of healing evangelism that took place in synagogue services.

Mark tells us that Jesus "traveled throughout Galilee, preaching in their synagogues and driving out demons" (1:39). But if he says Jesus preached in synagogues, he does *not* say Jesus drove out demons there.

When Jesus preached in the synagogue at Capernaum, however, His sermon was interrupted by an outburst from a demonized man, and Jesus responded by immediately ordering the spirit out (Mark 1:21–26; Luke 4:33–35). This, too, was an unplanned event, one that led to a positive response: "The people were all so amazed that they asked each other, 'What is this? A new teaching—and with authority! He even gives orders to evil spirits and they obey him'" (Mark 1:27).

A healing in another synagogue was not so well received.

The religious establishment in Galilee was upset because Jesus and His disciples were not following their rules about the Sabbath. He had the gall to declare Himself "Lord of the Sabbath" (Matthew 12:8; Mark 2:28; Luke 6:5). Right afterward He preached in the synagogue (Luke 6:6), where He invited a man with a withered hand to come forward during the sermon.

The question in the Pharisees' mind, of course, was whether it was lawful to heal on the Sabbath. "But Jesus . . . said to the man with the shriveled hand, 'Get up and stand in front of everyone.' So he got up and stood there" (Luke 6:8). Jesus then healed the man publicly before the entire congregation, prompting a response from the authorities: "They were furious and began to discuss with one another what they might do to Jesus" (Luke 6:11).

There are New Testament precedents, then, for healing during church services, even Sabbath (or Lord's Day) services, since Jesus did it on at least two occasions. There is also a precedent for causing the leaders to become furious if the healing contradicts their traditions.

Introducing Healing to Church Services

Although Sabbath traditions might not be a problem today, traditions about how "everything should be done in a fitting and orderly way" (1 Corinthians 14:40) sometimes are. The favorite slogan of many church boards is *It's never been done in our church before!* (One story, probably apocryphal, says that one board offered that as the reason for not commemorating the church's one hundredth anniversary!) My son, David, defines the tradition of our own denomination by saying, "It is Presbyterian to pray for the sick. It's just not Presbyterian for them to get better."

I have heard two very different ways suggested for minimizing opposition and introducing healing into any given church.

One suggestion is from Bob Whitaker, a Presbyterian minister who, with Doug McMurry, has written a privately circulated syllabus for seminars on renewal (*Equipping for Congregational Renewal*, Presbyterian & Reformed Renewal Ministries, International, n.d.). He writes:

> In the early seventies, I was an associate in a large church. I wanted to pray for the sick publicly with the laying on of hands, but it seemed unlikely that it would ever be allowed. I let my convictions be known periodically and committed

> the matter to the Lord in prayer. Then one day my senior pastor returned from a trip, impressed by another church's healing ministry. He invited me to draw up a proposal for the study of the healing ministry and its possible implementation. I did, and after polishing it in staff, we presented it to our elders. As a consequence, they okayed a committee, composed mostly of medical people, to study the healing movement. They spent a year reading books on healing, visiting healing services in different kinds of churches, interviewing persons active in healing ministries, and talking with those who had experienced healing. They were so impressed that they went back to the elders and recommended the commencement of monthly Sunday night communion and healing services with the laying on of hands by ministers and elders. The proposal went through without a ripple and was readily accepted with growing blessing for the church. Also, other churches started following our example.

Another suggestion for introducing healing into churches comes from C. Peter Wagner in his book *How to Have a Healing Ministry in Any Church* (Regal, 1988). Wagner does not recommend making healing ministry an up-front issue requiring lengthy study by the elders, nor does he insist on holding specific services for healing. In fact, he calls for nothing new in the church—only doing it better:

> Praying for the sick is already a part of the ministry of every church I know. What is the problem then? The problem is that not many sick people who are prayed for are perceived to be healed as a direct result of the prayers. The power released through praying for the sick in most churches leaves a great deal to be desired. Here is where I hope we can see some measurable improvement in the days to come.

Wagner reports on the development of healing ministry in the church to which he belongs, Lake Avenue Congregational Church in Pasadena. It started in his own Sunday school class while they were studying Acts. Prayer ministry was taught and class time given to prayer ministry. Soon a class prayer team was formed that ministered for an hour every Sunday morning in the church prayer chapel. Eventually the pastor appointed a church prayer team to pray with people after services:

> At the end of each service, Pastor [Paul] Cedar invites those who need prayer for healing and anything else to go out a certain door leading to the prayer room after the service is dismissed. There the prayer team ministers to them, and numerous cases of healing have been reported.

Models of Church Ministry

If your church is preaching the Gospel, then adding healing ministry produces healing evangelism. There are many different models of the way healing can be added to the regular ministry of the church. Here are some examples:

- Prayer teams may offer prayer ministry at special times (as in Glendale, mentioned in chapter 1) or following regular services (as in Pasadena).
- The front pew of the sanctuary may be roped off for special prayer by the elders, as at Hollywood (Calif.) Presbyterian Church. At the conclusion of services there, the pastor, the Rev. Lloyd Ogilvie, invites those who want prayer and anointing with oil to come forward. The prayer session with the elders takes place immediately after the benediction.
- Special services may be held specifically for healing. Bob Whitaker holds monthly Sunday night services for communion and healing. Our Lord's Community Church (Reformed Church in America) in Oklahoma City, according to Peter Wagner in *How to Have a Heal-*

> *ing Ministry in Any Church*, schedules and advertises its regular Sunday evening services as healing services. "They call it The Fellowship of the Healing Christ," writes Wagner, "and use a fairly structured liturgy as an order of service. The word is out around the community, and many people, even from other churches, come for prayer or bring sick friends and relatives to be healed."

Many churches will not be open to any of these models, at least not right away. Prayer and patience are necessary. You need sensitivity to the Spirit in order to know what may be done in your church and how it may be introduced. In some cases there may be opposition from unexpected sources. But in many churches, as in those above, a healing ministry may eventually be met with enthusiasm and success.

As difficult as it is to get some churches to open up to the idea of healing ministry in the Church, it can be even more difficult for people to accept the idea of healing evangelism in mass crusades. Most of us today are uncomfortable with this format. Are there ways of doing healing evangelism in crusades that are appropriate for us traditional evangelical types?

I believe there are, and we will consider them in the next chapter.

17

Compassion and Healing for a Large Crowd

Jesus was not a carpenter, at least not after beginning His public ministry. He was a full-time itinerant preacher supported by the offerings of friends (Luke 8:1–3). Specifically, Jesus was a healing evangelist. Most of His evangelism, judging from the New Testament, took place in meetings with large crowds. Really, then, He was a mass healing evangelist, the forerunner of those who preach and heal in large crusades today.

I am a mass evangelist, too. But for many years I was skeptical of healing evangelism. My skepticism was due to what little I knew of healing crusades by Pentecostals, and that was mainly what I saw on television. Such crusades appeared to be sensationalist and man-glorifying—spectacular performances designed to impress the crowd with the wonder-working powers of the star evangelist. By glorifying man, they diminished the honor of Christ. The "miracle cures" were displays that could easily be faked by a good showman. The crusades appeared to be heavily commercialized. The evangelists seemed intent not on offering Christ but on taking the money of the people.

I was really turned off.

When one prominent Pentecostal evangelist came to Pensacola's Bayfront Auditorium, I sat in the front of the balcony where I could see clearly what was happening. I expected at least to hear a good salvation message preached. I was disappointed. The evangelist started to preach, but within minutes, even before getting through his introduction, he announced that the power of the Spirit was on him so heavily that he would have to dispense with the sermon and move immediately to laying hands on people. For quite some time he did so, and I saw nothing significant happen except for a few people speaking in tongues.

Positive Examples

Over the years my skepticism has been mitigated somewhat by the realization that, although there are many phonies, there are also a good number of genuine healing evangelists trying to bring people to Christ, and not glorify themselves or line their own pockets. In the ministries of these evangelists, genuine healing miracles take place.

Peterson Sozi

The person who has had the most significant impact in convincing me of the legitimacy of healing evangelism is the Rev. Peterson Sozi. I have stayed in his home on most of my eleven trips to Uganda. He has often stayed in mine. He has become one of my dearest friends.

As a Christian from the two-thirds world, Peterson finds it easier to believe in divine intervention and miracles than I do from the West. He sees many healings and other miracles as a result of his ministry. His great desire is to bring people to salvation in Christ, and he hates anything that interferes with that goal. He is troubled by the fact that many people are more concerned with healing than with salvation. Many who have come to his crusades have professed Christ, received a miracle healing and then disappeared. Their profession was not genuine; once they had their healing, they had all they wanted. They felt no further need to go to crusade services and certainly not to go to church.

Thus, although prayer for the sick is often part of Peterson's crusade services, he downplays it so that it does not divert attention from the more important issue of salvation.

Delores Winder

Another significant influence for me has been Delores Winder, the Presbyterian laywoman whose retreat center, Shepherd's Pasture, I mentioned in chapter 15.

Delores suffered for nearly twenty years from pseudoarthrosis, a medically incurable bone disease. For fifteen years she was confined to a body cast. She received four spinal fusions, none of which was permanently successful. Finally the doctors performed two percutaneous cordotomies. This irreversible procedure, burning the nerve centers in the base of the brain to sever spinal cord segments, is performed only on terminal patients in order to relieve their pain. After these surgeries Delores no longer had feeling in most of her body and could not control bodily functions.

As time went on one of her kidneys shut down and the other became badly infected. Her esophagus ruptured and her bowels did not move for weeks. She was close to death. In fact, she and her husband, Bill, were making funeral arrangements when friends insisted they attend a Kathryn Kuhlman service.

Delores went to the meeting very sick and very skeptical. But during a fifteen-minute period in that service in 1975 she was completely healed. Not only was the disease cured (a healing that was later medically verified), but the irreversible results of her surgeries had been reversed. Feeling was restored, along with the control of bodily functions. And Delores could walk freely. She is a walking medical miracle.

I had long believed that flamboyant evangelists like Kuhlman were all fake. But as I got to know Delores, I could not deny the validity of her miracle. Today, almost twenty years after her healing, she is a spry and energetic lady. Now she travels to churches with Bill to speak about healing and to pray for the sick in her own ministry as a healing evangelist. Their ministry is the very opposite of flamboyance.

Richard Roberts

In 1993 I was on a team conducting a crusade in Trivandrum, India. The main speaker was Richard Roberts, son of Oral Roberts and heir to the Roberts evangelistic empire. Even though I had my own ministry by that time as a healing evangelist, I had not overcome my skepticism of the Roberts ministry and others like it. I knew there were many genuine, humble healing evangelists like Peterson and Delores, but I was still uncertain (for good reason) about those in the evangelistic major leagues.

The Trivandrum crusade was interdenominational, with charismatic Roman Catholics and the ecumenical Church of South India participating. Most of the team of American evangelists were Pentecostals from Oral Roberts University. I was the token non-Pentecostal. I was helping to teach in the training seminars for pastors every day; but in the evangelistic rallies every night I had no function except to sit on the platform—which gave me an opportunity to observe carefully. I also had the opportunity to observe the team members behind the scenes, including at dinner after the crusade each night in the dining room of our hotel.

One evening a team member from ORU had a word of knowledge describing a woman who was being healed at that moment. The team member pointed to the section of the crusade grounds where she was seated. He mentioned her age and described the illness from which she was being healed. Almost immediately a woman from where he had pointed came to the platform and said she was the person. Her age, she said, had been given exactly. She indeed had the very illness he had described but could feel that she had been immediately healed.

A few years before, if I had seen such a thing on TV or even from the audience, I would have been sure the woman was a "plant." But at dinner that evening after the service there was amazement and rejoicing over the precise accuracy of the word of knowledge. Clearly if the woman was a plant, it was unknown to any of the team members, including Richard himself.

I am sure it was a miracle. Everything I saw and heard during that week seemed genuine.

Warnings

Still, though there are many legitimate healing evangelists, mass evangelism is capable of abuse and has suffered abuse. I am still skeptical of much that I see on TV. Whether miracles are faked or real, it is always wrong when an evangelist talks more about giving money than about receiving the Lord, or when he calls more attention to himself than to Christ.

Our calling is to bring people to Christ. Following the biblical pattern for evangelism means praying for the sick and demonstrating Christ's compassion. When this is done in the power of the Spirit, many will be supernaturally healed.

It honors the Lord and encourages faith in those present when persons who are healed are allowed to testify. Our task is not to provide proof that will overwhelm and convince the skeptic, and there will always be those who suspect us of fakery and will imagine every genuine testimony to be a plant. An important part of our task is to be humble and genuine, honoring Christ and attracting persons to Him.

We must take care not to boast about healings. Jesus made no claims about His miracle cures. The results spoke for themselves and word got around about what had been done. On several occasions Jesus even asked those who had been cured not to tell anyone (for example, in Matthew 12:16), apparently because He was already overwhelmed with crowds of people coming for healing and because He needed no more word-of-mouth advertising!

Boastful claims do more than destroy the humility that the Gospel is supposed to demonstrate. They give false hopes. I have often seen posters and handbills proclaiming, "Come see the sick healed, the lame walk and the blind receive sight! Come receive your personal miracle!" This is an outgrowth of the faulty theology that says, "Every sick person here will be healed, and if you are not healed it is your own fault for not having enough faith."

I want to give hope but not false hope. I know that the Kingdom is here and yet not yet. I know that God in His sovereignty will heal some and leave others temporarily unhealed. So when I invite the sick to come for prayer I say, "I believe that some today will receive a healing touch from Jesus. You may be one of them." I try not to promise too much and not to claim too much.

Models for Compassion

Jesus should be our model in healing evangelism. We read, "When Jesus . . . saw a large crowd, he had compassion on them and healed their sick" (Matthew 14:14). The motive for healing is compassion. The occasion of the compassion is seeing the large crowd.

Many Scriptures summarize Jesus' ministry with emphasis on His healing ministry to the crowds. Here are just a few examples:

> Jesus went throughout Galilee, teaching in their synagogues, preaching the good news of the kingdom, and healing every disease and sickness among the people. News about him spread all over Syria, and people brought to him all who were ill with various diseases, those suffering severe pain, the demon-possessed, the epileptics and the paralytics, and he healed them. Large crowds from Galilee, the Decapolis, Jerusalem, Judea and the region across the Jordan followed him.
>
> Matthew 4:23–25

> Great crowds came to him, bringing the lame, the blind, the crippled, the dumb and many others, and laid them at his feet; and he healed them. The people were amazed when they saw the dumb speaking, the crippled made well, the lame walking and the blind seeing. And they praised the God of Israel.
>
> Matthew 15:30–31

> Many followed him, and he healed all their sick.
>
> Matthew 12:15

> The blind and the lame came to him at the temple, and he healed them.
>
> Matthew 21:14

> And everywhere he went—into villages, towns or countryside—they placed the sick in the marketplaces. They begged him to let them touch even the edge of his cloak, and all who touched him were healed.
>
> Mark 6:56

> When the sun was setting, the people brought to Jesus all who had various kinds of sickness, and laying his hands on each one, he healed them.
>
> Luke 4:40

We see the same pattern of ministry in the book of Acts among those who had been discipled by Jesus and those who had been discipled by the disciples. Note this description of Philip's ministry:

> Philip went down to a city in Samaria and proclaimed the Christ there. When the crowds heard Philip and saw the miraculous signs he did, they all paid close attention to what he said. With shrieks, evil spirits came out of many, and many paralytics and cripples were healed. So there was great joy in that city.
>
> Acts 8:5–8

Here is a description of a healing by Paul in a preaching situation before a crowd:

> In Lystra there sat a man crippled in his feet, who was lame from birth and had never walked. He listened to Paul as he was speaking. Paul looked directly at him, saw that he had faith to be healed and called out, "Stand up on your

> feet!" At that, the man jumped up and began to walk. When the crowd saw what Paul had done, they shouted. . . .
>
> Acts 14:8–11

Presently there is renewed interest in healing within denominational churches, especially those involved in the charismatic renewal. Most of this interest centers on healing in a church context, in services or small group meetings. The focus is pastoral and ecclesiastical. This is healing but not healing evangelism.

Traditional churches do little in the way of mass evangelism. They do almost no healing evangelism in connection with mass evangelism. That field is left to our Pentecostal brothers and sisters, perhaps in reaction to the style of healing evangelism done by Pentecostal mass evangelists.

There is great need for non-Pentecostals to grasp the reality that healing evangelism is biblical. Obedience to Scripture as well as compassion for the sick and the desire to win people to Christ should motivate us to begin using healing evangelism in outreach to the multitudes. If we do not lean toward a Pentecostal style, let us develop our own methods and strategies. I hope this book will encourage many to try.

Methods in Large Crusades

Let's consider some methods that can be used to pray for the sick in mass meetings.

General Prayer for All the Sick

The first and most basic method is to have general prayer for all the sick. The evangelist invites the sick to raise their hands while he or she prays a general healing prayer for all those with upraised hands, and names various diseases they might have. (Some evangelists invite people, instead of raising their hands, to lay their hands, when appropriate, on the parts of their bodies that need healing.)

In many mass situations, a general prayer is often the only way to pray for everyone. But it lacks the element of touch that is basic to much New Testament healing, except in the sense that the sick in this latter case lay hands on themselves. (I can think of no scriptural example of having the sick lay hands on themselves.)

A Healing Line

A second method is to have a healing line. Those in need of prayer line up and the evangelist walks down the line laying hands on each one. Sometimes the evangelist stays in one place and the line walks by him as he lays on hands. Sometimes anointing with oil is done along with, or instead of, the laying on of hands.

The healing line is a method I use. It follows a general prayer for all the sick, whom I have invited to come forward and are standing or sitting in a line across the front. My prayer invites the healing power of Christ and asks that, as I touch each person in His name, He will touch him or her, too. After the prayer I walk down the line, lay my hands on the head of each one and say, "Be healed and set free in Jesus' name." After the last one has been touched, I pray another prayer that the healing power of Christ will remain on each one until he or she is healed.

Following this, I invite those who believe they have received a healing touch from Jesus to testify. Many do so. Most often they speak of pain or fever leaving them. Some demonstrate that they now have new freedom in the use of formerly crippled or impaired limbs. Some speak of a sudden improvement in vision.

After some testimonies, I speak to those who have not been immediately and completely healed. I point out that Jesus often takes time to heal, and give some illustrations from the New Testament (which we discussed in chapter 3). I tell them that they should not be discouraged but continue to plead with Jesus for their healing. And then I remind them that "your healing will come in His time and according to His will."

This is generally the best way, I believe, to minister to the sick in mass meetings. It incorporates not only prayer but the element of individual touch (one of the action prayers we discussed in chapter 11), which the New Testament stresses.

Words of Knowledge

A third method to minister to the sick in mass meetings, the method connected earlier with Richard Roberts, is the word of knowledge.

During our time together in Trivandrum, Richard told me that he prefers this method to the healing line used by his father, who often spent hours laying hands on one person after another in a healing line that might include thousands.

Richard offers a general prayer for all the sick, then invites the Holy Spirit to show him whom He is healing at that time. Impressions come to him and he speaks them out. Often, as in the incident I narrated, individuals emerge from the congregation testifying that they are the ones being described and that they are indeed being healed.

The principal reason I have not used this method is that the Holy Spirit has not given me these impressions. If He did, and if I were sure they were from Him, I would speak them out. On the other hand, one reason the Holy Spirit has not given me these impressions may be that I have not sought them. I prefer to work in other ways.

I can find no examples in Scripture of words of knowledge being used in healing ministry, although this does not mean they were not used in New Testament times or that they are inappropriate for today. But I have doubts as to whether this phenomenon is what Paul had in mind when he referred to "the word of knowledge by the same Spirit" (1 Corinthians 12:8, KJV).

In the epistle Paul was contrasting the wisdom and knowledge that come from the Holy Spirit with the wisdom and knowledge of the world. He wrote:

> We do, however, speak a message of wisdom among the mature, but not the wisdom of this age or of the rulers of this age, who are coming to nothing. . . . We have not received the spirit of the world but the Spirit who is from God, that we may understand what God has freely given us. This is what we speak, not in words taught us by human wisdom but in words taught by the Spirit, expressing spiritual truths in spiritual words.
>
> 1 Corinthians 2:6, 12–13

In that setting he said:

> To one there is given through the Spirit the message of wisdom, to another the message of knowledge by means of the same Spirit.
>
> 1 Corinthians 12:8

It appears that Paul had in mind something generally more profound than the description of a person and his symptoms.

While the use of words of knowledge in healing evangelism means that you do not need to spend a long time with a healing line, it also means that no one receives a personal healing touch from the evangelist or one of his associates. As there are only a limited number of people you can call out from your audience in this way, so there may be only a small number of persons healed in this way.

Also, the use of words of knowledge is easily sensationalized. It can degenerate into something like the performance of a stage magician amazing the crowd with a marvelous knowledge of facts he seemingly could not know naturally. Anything that draws attention and wonder to the evangelist can easily detract from Christ. We want people to be amazed and marvel at Him, not us. This is another reason this method should be used only cautiously.

Multiple Lines

There is a fourth solution to the problem of one evangelist having to lay hands on thousands of people. Why should one person do all the work? Why not have several prayer lines, each with its own evangelist or prayer team?

I have used this approach, as I said earlier, in large meetings in Uganda. After my sermon I announce that there will be prayer for the sick. Then I point out different prayer stations at different locations around the area. At each station is a prayer team to pray and lay hands on all who come.

There are several variations on the method of multiple prayer teams. Some evangelists have separate healing lines for separate ailments. At least one, an evangelist in Argentina where many are demonized by occult activity, has a special tent where demonized persons can go for deliverance.

John Wimber has people stand who are in need of healing; then prayer teams go to them. Sometimes he asks all those with a particular ailment to stand.

Once when a friend of mine was in the congregation, Wimber had those with back problems stand. Then he invited those sitting near them to pray for them. My friend stood. He had a congenital back problem and had not had a good night's sleep all his life because he was awakened frequently by pain. That evening, as those around him prayed for him, he felt something move and adjust in his back. The next morning he told me he had had the first good night's sleep of his life and considered himself about ninety percent healed. I saw his wife about six months later. She said he was still sleeping well and was still ninety percent healed.

Falling under the Power

It used to trouble me to see people fall to the floor as they were being prayed for. I first saw this on television and heard that Pentecostals called it "being slain in the Spirit"—which makes it sound like a judgment. Now I know it can be a great blessing (even though the term *slain in the Spirit* is offensive to me and is certainly unbiblical). But at first I opposed the practice strongly and considered it the work of evil spirits. I had to rethink my position in light of Scripture and in light of the fact that it sometimes happened in my own meetings at times when the Holy Spirit was moving powerfully.

As I pray for people and the power of the Holy Spirit comes on them, some become weak and fall to the floor. The Lord often seems to do much healing, especially emotional and spiritual healing, as they are resting under the power of the Spirit. I am no longer surprised by this or opposed to it and recognize that the Lord heals people while they are in this resting mode. They often testify later that they felt the power of the Spirit come on them with such heaviness that they could no longer stand. They felt overwhelmed by the presence of the Lord.

Falling under the power has historical precedents, especially in the revivals under George Whitefield and John

Wesley. And there are several examples in Scripture of persons being so overwhelmed by the presence of the Lord that they could no longer stand. Among them:

> . . . This was the appearance of the likeness of the glory of the LORD. When I saw it, I fell facedown, and I heard the voice of one speaking.
>
> Ezekiel 1:28

> Then I heard him speaking, and as I listened to him, I fell into a deep sleep, my face to the ground.
>
> Daniel 10:9

> When the disciples heard [the voice of the Lord speaking while a cloud enveloped them], they fell facedown to the ground, terrified.
>
> Matthew 17:6

> His appearance was like lightning, and his clothes were white as snow. The guards were so afraid of him that they shook and became like dead men.
>
> Matthew 28:3–4

> When Jesus said, "I am he," they drew back and fell to the ground.
>
> John 18:6

> As he neared Damascus on his journey, suddenly a light from heaven flashed around him. He fell to the ground and heard a voice say to him, "Saul, Saul, why do you persecute me?"
>
> Acts 9:3–4

> When I saw him, I fell at his feet as though dead.
>
> Revelation 1:17

A particularly remarkable passage appears in 1 Kings 8:11 and 2 Chronicles 5:14. Solomon had built his Temple and the priests had brought the Ark of the Covenant and set it up in the Holy of Holies. Then the cloud of the *shekinah* glory of the presence of the Lord came and filled the Temple. The priests were unable to stand to perform their service in the presence of God's glory. (Unhappily the NIV fails to translate *amad*, the ordinary Hebrew word for *stand*. All other translations I consulted render 1 Kings 8:11 similar to the King James: "The priests could not stand to minister because of the cloud: for the glory of the LORD had filled the house of the LORD.")

The phenomenon of falling under the power, when it occurs, creates certain problems.

One is that many Christians are unfamiliar with it and react negatively (as I once did). Nor do they like to see it take place in their church sanctuaries, since they consider it disorderly—or downright demonic. Sometimes I explain, before praying for the sick, that this might happen and, if so, not to be alarmed. I try to set everyone at ease by saying that it is a normal (though not conventional) experience and that, if the Lord chooses to work this way, who are we to object?

A more serious problem is that this phenomenon can be sensationalized. Some evangelists give the impression that they personally possess great power so that they are able to merely touch a person, or wave toward him, or even blow on him, and he will fall over. We must be careful of anything that may draw attention away from the Lord.

Compassion

Let me conclude this chapter where I began it—with a reference to the compassion of Jesus. Compassion is the reason Jesus healed. It should be a major reason for our healing ministries as well. When I see the sick, I want to pray for them and touch them in the hope that Jesus will use that action prayer to bring healing to them. It is not compassionate to ignore their suffering and neglect to pray.

All our methods of healing evangelism must reflect and demonstrate the compassion of Christ, toward the end that individuals may not only be healed but embrace His compassion as it was shown at Calvary. Healing is not an end in itself but a means of bringing people to Christ and salvation.

In the final chapter of this book, I will offer some suggestions for you to get started in your own ministry of healing evangelism.

Part 6

Getting Started

You want to strengthen your witness with effective prayer for the sick. You have even read this book! Where do you go from here?

18

Your Ministry of Healing Evangelism

I hope by now you are convinced that compassionate, effective prayer for the sick should be an important component of Christian evangelism, as it was for Jesus, the Twelve, the 72 and the early Church. I hope you are beginning to understand how you can use the power and gifts of the Holy Spirit to have this kind of ministry. And I expect you are beginning to think through ways that healing prayer can be integrated into the life of your church and the other ministries with which you are involved. Perhaps you are considering the models of the Yoido Full Gospel Church and the Glendale Presbyterian Church, or perhaps you are considering some other models more appropriate to your own situation.

In this the last chapter of the book, I want to suggest practical steps you can take in getting started in a ministry of healing prayer for yourself and for your church.

Following this chapter are three appendixes that deal with theological issues: "Should Positive Confession

Replace Prayer?", "Is Healing a Dangerous Fad?" and "The Gifts and Guidance of the Spirit in the Reformed Tradition." If you are not troubled about these issues yourself, you will certainly encounter people who are! I have also included a listing of resources for you to use as you start moving into the ministry of healing evangelism, and a bibliography of recommended books that will be helpful as you develop your ministry.

Your Private Prayer Life

We have already noted that "Jesus often withdrew to lonely places and prayed" (Luke 5:16) and that, as a result, "the power of the Lord was present for him to heal the sick" (verse 17). The foundation of Jesus' effectiveness in public healing was His life of private prayer.

Private prayer must be the foundation of your healing ministry, too. You cannot expect to be more effective praying in public than you are praying in private. The first step toward developing a ministry of healing evangelism, then, is developing your private prayer life. You should not seek a ministry of healing prayer for others without first laying a good foundation in your own experience and habits of private prayer.

I also hope you will never be entirely satisfied with your prayer life. You should always want to go deeper.

When to Pray?

Here is our model: "Very early in the morning, while it was still dark, Jesus got up, left the house and went off to a solitary place, where he prayed" (Mark 1:35). Some believers point to that verse as a rule for all of us. Should it be a rule for me? Am *I* required to get up very early every morning? What if I'm a night person?

It may be that Jesus rose very early that morning for a special time of prayer before embarking on a new evangelistic journey to the nearby villages (verse 38). Nevertheless, it is clear that such times of prayer, more exceptional for us, were common for Jesus and that frequent prayer characterized His daily life.

Many find a morning prayer time to be the most profitable because their minds are not yet full of the distractions of the day. Night people, on the other hand, find the night hours the most profitable, not only because they are at their best but because others have gone to bed and will leave them alone.

In any case, it is biblical to have stated times of prayer every day. "Three times a day [Daniel] got down on his knees and prayed, giving thanks to his God" (Daniel 6:10). The psalmist cried out to God "evening, morning and noon" (Psalm 55:17). That should challenge us!

Where to Pray?

Jesus often prayed in solitary places. Judas knew he would find Jesus in Gethsemane because that is where He went regularly to pray.

There are at least two reasons Jesus sought solitary places to pray. First, so that He would not be disturbed. Second, which we may infer from Hebrews 5:7 ("He offered up prayers and petitions with loud cries and tears to the one who could save him"), so that His prayers would not disturb others.

Find a solitary place for prayer and discipline yourself to go there regularly.

Special Times of Prayer

From time to time, set aside extended periods for concentrating on prayer. It is good to devote a whole day to prayer and fasting. There are many examples of this in Scripture.

Many days I have little time to spend with my wife or I am away, so at other times I will set aside everything else to spend extended time with her. It is the same with the Lord. He, too, should receive extended times of special attention. You need those times to get to know Him better.

Listening in Prayer

It is important in your prayer times to listen for the Lord as well as speak to Him. Sensitivity to the leading of the Spirit is the key element in praying effectively for the sick. Allow Him to direct your private prayer times. Develop sensitivity to the Spirit when you are praying alone, and you will be able to perceive His leading when you are praying for others.

Using the Gifts

Many gifts of the Spirit operate in personal prayer times as well as in corporate settings. Develop these gifts in private so that you can move in them freely at other times.

Your Corporate Prayer Life

The Bible stresses the importance of corporate prayer. Jesus sought, for example, to have the disciples pray with Him (Matthew 26:36–38).

Prayer Partners

Once you have begun to develop your private prayer life, find at least one other person with whom you can pray frequently. You will help each other and your agreement will strengthen your prayers (Matthew 18:19–20).

A Prayer Group

Look for a prayer group that meets regularly and shares your interest and concerns in prayer. There may be such a group in your church, or groups in your community that meet in homes and include people from several churches.

In many churches, regrettably, what is still called a "prayer meeting" has become a service for Bible study and preaching with little prayer; and the brief periods of prayer are cold and formal. Perhaps in time the Lord will enable you to bring renewal to *your* church prayer meeting.

Prayer Ministry

It is good if you can find a group that not only prays together but does prayer ministry with healing prayer. How wonderful if you can find believers who pray as they do in the cells in the Yoido Church, where members lay hands on one another and minister in prayer for one another's needs!

Many prayer groups have become prayer teams to which persons in need come for prayer ministry. Some churches, like the one in Glendale, have designated prayer teams to do prayer ministry at the conclusion of services or other stated times.

Your own ministry of healing evangelism will get off to its best start as you participate in such a prayer team.

Your Involvement in Larger Fellowships

As you grow in prayer and prayer ministry, you will soon need to avail yourself of resources outside your immediate community. There are many organizations that offer training seminars, retreats, conferences, literature and other assistance.

Appendix 4 on pp. 248–50 lists some of these organizations. They are of two types:

Renewal Service Committees

One kind of organization is the "renewal service committee" that offers a variety of services for those in a particular denominational tradition. The gifts and power of the Holy Spirit are interpreted in ways consistent with the theology of that tradition. Worship is conducted in familiar ways. And participants in conferences, sharing a common heritage, are comfortable with one another. You may want to relate first to the renewal service committee for your denominational tradition.

Since the one I know best is Presbyterian & Reformed Renewal Ministries International, I have listed some of the services it offers as examples of the kinds of services offered by most of these committees:

- "Dunamis" retreats are intensive leadership training seminars, each on a specific topic. They include lectures, times of prayer, worship and discussion, as well as laboratory periods to practice what you are learning.
- "Harvest School of Prayer" offers instruction in prayer through literature and seminars.
- "Prayer Mountains" are prayer retreats, not to learn about prayer but to do the work of prayer. I mentioned them in chapter 15.
- Regional conferences, ranging from one day to a week, feature workshop periods, small group prayer meetings and worship periods led by gifted worship leaders.
- "Spirit Alive" is a program for congregational renewal. A lay witness team and preacher are invited to hold a variety of meetings on a particular theme and emphasis at a church over several days.
- Short-term mission trips provide the opportunity for teams from the U.S. to go to other countries to minister renewal. PRRMI hopes eventually to have teams from other countries come here.
- Literature includes the quarterly magazine, *Renewal News*, and cassette tapes, mainly of messages from PRRMI conferences.

Every group differs, but I hope you will contact the renewal service committee for your denomination and begin to avail yourself of their resources.

Specialized Organizations

The second category of organizations that will enrich your prayer ministry is one that offers specialized services to Christians from many traditions. Some groups, for example, focus on healing, with conferences and literature on healing available to all.

Check appendix 4 for the addresses of some of these organizations.

Your Investment in Others

As you grow in prayer and prayer ministry and as you learn from others, you will soon be able to teach others what you have learned yourself. In fact, your own growth rate will increase when you are giving out as well as taking in.

Home Groups

You may want to form a group in your home, or join a group that already exists, to pray for one another and do prayer ministry. This group may well develop into a prayer team to which others will turn. Be especially prayerful and sensitive to the Spirit as you form and develop this ministry.

Cautions for Home Groups

There are some dangers to avoid. Someone may want to come to the group for the purpose of dominating and taking over. The group may develop an exclusive spirit and criticize those who do not participate. Leaders in your church may be suspicious or even hostile, suspecting your group of divisive intentions.

If you are aware of these dangers, you can usually avoid them. Don't be discouraged. The enemy wants to sow confusion where the Lord is working, but that should encourage you all the more to be sure you are doing the Lord's work in the Lord's way.

Your Involvement in Your Church

Some churches have integrated healing prayer effectively into the life of the church. (Examples were given in chapter 16.) This is as it should be. Healing should be as normal a part of the evangelism of the Church as it was in the first century.

Many churches are far from this, however, and yours may be one of them. What can you do?

Offer Suggestions

Whatever you do or suggest should be done in as nonthreatening a way as possible. Many churches are frightened by the idea of healing services and absolutely panicked by deliverance! All, however, believe in prayer. It is better to suggest a prayer meeting than a healing service.

Do nothing until you have been a positive, active member of the church for some time. Only after the leaders of your church are convinced of your wisdom, spiritual maturity and constructive attitude will they be open to your suggestions about prayer ministry. It is especially important to gain the confidence of your pastor.

Study the church to see where prayer ministry might be introduced most naturally—perhaps in a prayer group or adult Sunday school class. (You might begin by having the group study this book. After weeks of reading and discussing, it may be ready to start doing healing evangelism.)

Is there a church prayer meeting? If not, encourage the start of one. If there is one already, then they already give time praying for the sick and those in need of healing. Perhaps they will be open to the idea of having a few people surround the person in need of healing, when he or she is present, and lay hands on him or her while the congregation prays.

Turn to the Elders

Does your church have elders? Have they ever discussed James 5:14–15 about the elders praying for the sick and anointing them with oil? How do they interpret that passage? How would they respond if someone from the congregation actually called on them? Once the elders—the ones to take the leadership in introducing prayer ministry to the congregation—have begun prayer ministry for the sick, they may not be so threatened when others do it, too.

Starting Your Ministry

In time, word will get around that you enjoy praying for the sick, and even that you have seen some persons healed in remarkable ways. Before long people will be coming to you for prayer and you will be praying for them, sometimes alone and sometimes with your prayer team. *When you pray for unbelievers, evangelize.*

Your ministry is under way. How is it to be exercised? Primarily in the local church? In connection with your denomination's renewal service committee or some other agency? In cooperation with a particular evangelist or movement?

These are questions the Holy Spirit must answer. He is the one who must guide and develop your ministry.

Now you have finished the final chapter and are ready to get started. First, however, I encourage you to read the appendixes and consider the books in the bibliography.

They will open resources to you that will be helpful. The first three appendixes, as I said earlier, deal with theological issues related to healing evangelism. If you are not troubled about these issues, you will certainly encounter people who are. You will want to be informed.

Appendix 1

Should Positive Confession Replace Prayer?

Christians from many churches united with us in prayer when Eileen, my wife, gave birth in 1976 to a baby girl with serious congenital defects. I described in chapter 4 how believers from a Pentecostal church that taught positive confession theology told us they were "thanking God in advance for her healing"; and how after Joy Anne's death they told Eileen the baby would have survived if only she had had more faith.

A year after Joy Anne died the Lord provided for us to adopt Katy, a special needs child with cerebral palsy. My mother-in-law prayed for her healing several times in a prayer group she attended. Some in the group rebuked her for praying repeatedly for her new granddaughter. They told her it was sin to pray for anything more than once. They, too, were advocates of positive confession teaching.

What is this doctrine that hindered people in one church from praying earnestly for Joy Anne's healing and caused others to rebuke my mother-in-law for praying more than once for Katy's?

Everyone who seeks to have a ministry of healing evangelism needs to understand this movement that calls itself "positive confession" or "word of faith." Its critics call it "name-it-and-claim it."

Many who believe in positive confession will be drawn to your ministry of healing evangelism. But if they observe that you are praying for healing and not "claiming" it by faith, they will try to correct you and get onto prayer teams associated with your ministry so that they can do things "the right way."

Also, since proponents of positive confession have come to prominence, some Christians assume that if you call yourself a charismatic or believe in the manifestational gifts of the Spirit for today, you yourself must be a believer in positive confession. They also assume that almost everyone engaged in healing ministry must be doing so based on positive confession theology. The very fact that you are engaging in healing evangelism is sufficient to make them conclude that you hold to the tenets of this doctrine.

Neither of these assumptions is necessarily correct.

As a healing evangelist and believer in the gifts of the Spirit for today, I have made an effort first to understand positive confession, then to distance myself from it. I will try to lay out the major points, as I understand them, and then urge you to distance yourself from it, too.

What Is Positive Confession?

The theology of the positive confession movement is an outgrowth of the teaching of E. W. Kenyon, a man trained in the metaphysical movement that produced Christian Science and similar mind-cure cults. Kenyon was an evangelical enamored of Christian Science. "All that Christian Science lacks," he wrote, "is the blood of Jesus Christ." That quotation is taken from page 25 of an important book that explores the origins of the positive confession movement, *A Different Gospel* by D. R. McConnell (Hendrickson, 1988). Kenyon went on to develop a doctrine that would be evangelical and biblical in its foundation, teaching the blood of Christ—on top of which it would place the methodology of Christian Science.

Proponents of positive confession believe that God promises blessings, especially perfect health and prosperity, to all believers. The way to receive what is promised is simply to claim it by faith and believe it is yours. If you still feel sick, it means you do not yet have the "manifestation" of your healing. The symptoms of your illness are lies of the devil to keep you from believing in your healing. You must not say, "I feel sick," even in prayer to God, because that is a negative confession. That is to repeat a lie of the devil and express unbelief. Instead, confess positively—"I am healed; I feel great!"—because that expresses and strengthens faith, which is necessary to obtain the manifestation of your healing.

Confess Your Healing

Christian Science (the philosophical father of the positive confession movement) denies the reality of sin, pain, sickness and death. These are only illusions. When you are *apparently* suffering pain or sickness, you do not pray about them. Instead you recognize that they are not real. Believers in Christian Science do not pray, at least not in the biblical sense. In fact, they do not even believe in a personal God to whom one may pray. Rather, they engage in religious readings and other exercises to strengthen their realization that the things they seem to be suffering are not real.

Believers in positive confession, by contrast, accept the reality of sin, sickness, death and our need for the cleansing blood of Jesus Christ. But they reason that their sickness is not real, not because sickness is not real but because Jesus has healed them.

Word of faith proponents base their thinking, in part, on passages like the following:

> [Abraham] is our father in the sight of God, in whom he believed—the God who gives life to the dead and calls things that are not as though they were. . . . [Abraham] did not waver through unbelief regarding the promise of God. . . .
>
> Romans 4:17, 20

We are called, say our word of faith brothers and sisters, to follow Abraham's example and believe that God will bring forth life from the dead. In fact, we are to call things that are not as though they already were. If I am sick, I will confess that I am healed already.

Claim It in Faith

Positive confession advocates do not believe in repeating God's promises back to Him in prayer and pleading persistently until the answer comes. They believe in claiming by faith whatever they think He has promised and then believing it has been given already, even when it does not appear that it has.

What You Say Is What You Get

Believers in positive confession insist that what we speak in faith we will see manifested in the flesh—for good or ill:

> The tongue has the power of life and death, and those who love it will eat its fruit.
>
> Proverbs 18:21

> Whatever you ask for in prayer, believe that you *have received* it, and it will be yours.
>
> Mark 11:24, emphasis added

"Just Symptoms"

What if you are claiming healing but the symptoms of your illness continue? You are to believe, according to positive confession, that you were healed the moment you first claimed your healing, since "by his wounds we *are* healed" (Isaiah 53:5, emphasis added). The problem is that you simply have not received the manifestation of your healing yet.

There is a positive confession joke about a conversation between two Christians.

The first Christian says to the second Christian, "Sounds like you've got quite a cold."

The second one says, "This isn't a cold; I'm healed. These are just demonic symptoms."

The first one scratches his head, then says, "Boy, it's almost as bad as having the real thing, isn't it?"

Pray Just Once

Once you have prayed, even though the symptoms persist and the answer is not yet manifested, word of faith proponents consider it sin and unbelief to think you are not healed and continue to pray for your healing. Rather, you are to thank God for the healing that has already occurred—to see in the Spirit what the Word promises and wait patiently for its manifestation "in the natural."

Don't Pray the Problem

Positive confession means that you always speak positively, especially to God but even to one another. Claim the solution. Don't mention the problem; that brings on fear and saps or even destroys faith. In fact, to pray persistently for your need is tantamount to vain repetition.

Pray for something just once; then thank God for answering. Don't pray the problem; thank God for the solution.

Bible Praying

I appreciate the emphases of the positive confession movement on faith and Scripture. But any movement should be judged to a certain degree by the consequences it has for its disciples. And I have become convinced that positive confession is severely detrimental to the prayer lives of many Christians. It puts them under bondage so that they cannot pray as the Scripture teaches.

God gave by divine inspiration the book of Psalms to be the prayer book and hymnal for ancient Israel, and for the use of the whole Church of Jesus Christ through all ages. Its prayers are to become models for our own praying.

But if the Psalter is the model for our prayers, then we will pray very differently from the way taught by the positive confession school.

The psalmist prayed his problems. There is little reference to financial problems in the Psalter, probably because David, the author of many of the psalms, was a wealthy king untroubled by poverty. But David prayed often about wicked men who were his enemies. When he was a young man, Saul was pursuing him to take his life. When he was an older man, he had many political foes.

Many psalms mention problems, and many whole psalms are primarily complaints and discussions of problems. Consider the following problems:

Foes (Psalm 3:1–2)
Faintness, sickness and enemies (Psalm 6)
The arrogant and wicked (Psalm 10:1–13)
The wicked (Psalm 12)
Enemies (Psalm 13)
Evildoers (Psalm 14)
Suffering (Psalm 22)
Enemies, grief and bodily affliction (Psalm 31:9–13)
Enemies (Psalm 35)
Guilt, bodily affliction (Psalm 38, especially verses 5–10)
Enemies (Psalm 41:4–9)
Israel's defeat (Psalm 44:9–26)
Evildoers (Psalm 53)
The wicked (Psalm 55)
Slanderers (Psalm 56)
Evil men (Psalm 57:4, 6)
Evildoers (Psalm 58)
Enemies (Psalm 59)
The wicked (Psalm 64)
Pain and distress (Psalm 69)
Enemies (Psalm 70)
Enemies (Psalm 74)
The nations (Psalm 79)
Trouble, depression and near-death illness (Psalm 88)
Troubles (Psalm 89:38–51)
The wicked (Psalm 94)
Distress, physical affliction (Psalm 102:1–11)

Wicked men (Psalm 109)
Evil men (Psalm 140)
Desperate need (Psalm 142)

The psalmist confesses ill health, contrary to the teaching of positive confession. Although the bodily ailments he describes are related to spiritual problems like grief and conviction of guilt, they appear nevertheless to be real physical problems. He describes his ailments as follows:

> Be merciful to me, LORD, for I am faint;
> O LORD, heal me, for my bones are in agony.
>
> Psalm 6:2

> My strength fails because of my affliction,
> and my bones grow weak.
>
> Psalm 31:10

> My wounds fester and are loathsome. . . .
> My back is filled with searing pain;
> there is no health in my body.
> I am feeble and utterly crushed;
> I groan in anguish of heart.
>
> Psalm 38:5, 7–8

> My soul is full of trouble
> and my life draws near the grave.
> I am counted among those who go down to the pit;
> I am like a man without strength.
> I am set apart with the dead. . . .
>
> Psalm 88:3–5

> My days vanish like smoke;
> my bones burn like glowing embers.
> My heart is blighted and withered like grass;
> I forget to eat my food.

Because of my loud groaning
    I am reduced to skin and bones.

Psalm 102:3–5

Contrary to positive confession teaching to pray about something only once, the psalmist cries out to the Lord for things he has prayed about many times, and complains that the Lord is taking so long to answer. We read:

How long, O LORD, how long?

Psalm 6:3

How long, O LORD? Will you forget me forever?
    How long will you hide your face from me?
How long must I wrestle with my thoughts
and every day have sorrow in my heart?
How long will my enemy triumph over me?

Psalm 13:1–2

How long will the enemy mock you, O God?

Psalm 74:10

How long, O LORD? Will you be angry forever?
    How long will your jealousy burn like fire?

Psalm 79:5

How long will you defend the unjust
and show partiality to the wicked?

Psalm 82:2

Will you be angry with us forever?

Psalm 85:5

How long, O LORD? Will you hide yourself forever?
    How long will your wrath burn like fire?

Psalm 89:46

How long will the wicked, O LORD,
how long will the wicked be jubilant?

Psalm 94:3

The psalmist complains to the Lord about his problems. "Hear me, O God, as I voice my complaint," he says (64:1). He offers such complaints as these:

Awake, O LORD! Why do you sleep?
    Rouse yourself! Do not reject us forever.
Why do you hide your face
    and forget our misery and oppression?
We are brought down to the dust;
    our bodies cling to the ground.
Rise up and help us;
    redeem us because of your unfailing love.

Psalm 44:23–26

I cry aloud to the LORD;
    I lift up my voice to the LORD for mercy.
I pour out my complaint before him;
    before him I tell my trouble.

Psalm 142:1–2

The psalmist describes his prayer times by saying, "Evening, morning and noon I cry out in distress, and he hears my voice" (Psalm 55:17).

Instead of telling us not to pray our problems, he says, "Cast your cares on the LORD and he will sustain you" (Psalm 55:22).

Instead of confessing that his prayers have all been answered and need not be repeated, or instead of claiming his great privileges as a child of God, he confesses, "I am poor and needy; come quickly to me, O God" (Psalm 70:5).

There are other Bible prayers than those in the Psalter; and they, too, represent a much different style of praying than that of our word of faith friends. The book of Lamentations is a prayer by the prophet Jeremiah, who "prayed the problem" and offered "negative" rather than "positive" confession to the Lord. In fact, Lamentations is a book of complaints that Jeremiah prayed for a long time.

Here is just one example:

Why do you always forget us?
Why do you forsake us so long?
Restore us to yourself, O LORD, that we may return;
renew our days as of old
unless you have utterly rejected us
and are angry with us beyond measure.

Lamentations 5:20–22

The Prayers and Teachings of Jesus

The prayers and teachings of Jesus also contradict the teaching and practice of positive confession. Word of faith teachers do not deal faithfully, for example, with the obvious thrust of Jesus' stories of the man who came to his friend at midnight (Luke 11:5–10) and the importunate widow with the unjust judge (Luke 18:1–8).

The point of the first story is, "Ask and it will be given to you; seek and you will find; knock and the door will be opened to you" (Luke 11:9). Clearly Jesus is talking about persistence in asking and seeking and knocking. "Because of the man's persistence," Jesus said, "he will get up and give him as much as he needs" (verse 8).

To illustrate a positive confession approach, on the other hand, the man would have had to "claim" bread from his neighbor and thank him in advance for it, even while the neighbor was still in bed.

It is hard to understand how anyone can miss the point of the second story, the story of the persistent widow, when Jesus said, "There was a widow in that town who kept coming to him with the plea. . ." (Luke 18:3). Jesus quoted the judge as saying, "Because this widow keeps bothering me, I will see that she gets justice, so that she won't eventually wear me out with her coming!" (verse 5). Jesus said specifically that she came to him *per-*

sistently and that the judge recognized that it was her frequent comings that were wearing him out.

Luke introduces the story, moreover, by saying, "Jesus told his disciples a parable to show them that they should always pray and not give up" (18:1). The story was told not to teach boldness of faith but persistence in prayer. Jesus told this parable specifically to criticize those who would stop praying after coming once—the very thing some Christian teachers insist we must do.

Is praying for a request more than once "vain repetitions" (KJV) or "babbling like pagans" (Matthew 6:7)? How did Jesus Himself pray? Did He ever repeat Himself or did He pray about something only once?

In the Garden of Gethsemane Jesus made the same request three times. Matthew 26:44 says that He "prayed the third time, saying the same thing." Jesus was not against repetition in prayer, only against the empty babbling of pagans who think there is magic power in repeating meaningless phrases.

How did Jesus pray? The author of Hebrews tells us, "During the days of Jesus' life on earth, he offered up prayers and petitions with loud cries and tears" (Hebrews 5:7). But according to positive confession teaching, we are only to claim what is our right and proceed immediately to praising God that we have already received what is not yet manifest.

Quite a contrast with the example of Jesus.

Why Is This Movement Popular?

The positive confession movement reminds me of the story of the boy whose Sunday school teacher asked him to define faith. The child replied, "Faith is believing what you know isn't so."

I believe in claiming things from Satan. In the name of Jesus we *should* take back what does not belong to him. But I do not believe it is right to claim things from God. The psalmist did not claim His promises, but he did plead them.

Positive confession appears effective because it is manipulative. The leader manipulates sick people into confessing publicly that they are healed, regardless of how they feel. And many people are willing to accept these testimonies and believe in these healings under the power of the evangelist.

Positive confession forbids the very kind of prayer that is most natural to us: earnest, continuous pleading with God about our problems; pouring out our hearts to Him about our needs and urging Him to intervene; begging Him to help and, when He delays, crying out, "How long, O Lord?"

Not only does word of faith teaching forbid the prayer that is most natural for us, but it forbids many of the very prayers the Holy Spirit has given us in the Psalms and elsewhere, and that the Lord Jesus Christ demonstrated for us in Gethsemane and with "loud cries and tears" through His life on earth.

For this reason I call positive confession "the anti-prayer movement." It does not forbid prayer, of course, but it forbids much of the most important prayer taught in the Bible. It substitutes claiming for pleading, confession for asking, and praising God that the prayer is answered (when it does not appear to have been answered) for persistent asking until the answer comes. It substitutes a psychological method borrowed from mind-cure cults, especially Christian Science, for the method of prayer taught in the Word of God.

Why is this movement popular? Why has it so captivated some nondenominational charismatic churches that, for them, to be charismatic is to engage in positive confession rather than Bible praying?

The most common reason given for the popularity of this movement is its appeal to our greed and self-interest. It offers formulas that it says will give us instant wealth and instant perfect health.

But surely another reason is that it spares us the hard work of Bible praying. Positive confession does not urge us to plead persistently with God with loud crying and tears, but instead—in case we feel guilty for *not* praying that way—it assures us that persistent pleading is the wrong way to pray and is indeed a harmful expression of sinful unbelief. God is viewed, in effect, as a cosmic slot machine. The moment you drop in your coin, the product is automatically dispensed.

Thus, it appeals to a society that is not only greedy but demanding of instant gratification. Positive confession is a feel-good religion that tells us not to speak to God about our negative problems, but rather to rejoice in our (not-yet-manifest) solutions. Wrestling in prayer (Colossians 4:12) is no more.

Another factor in the popularity of this movement is obvious from the fact that it has gained ground among independent churches but not among the mainline denominational churches that participate in the charismatic renewal. That factor is ignorance of the Psalms. Except for a few favorites like Psalms 23 and 100, American Christians outside of denominational churches are largely ignorant of these models of godly prayer. Praise choruses based on isolated passages from the Psalter usually draw on verses of praise rather than complaint.

Denominational churches, on the other hand, continue to use the Psalter in their liturgies. Most services contain at least one reading from the Psalms, often a responsive reading in which the entire congregation participates. Some Episcopalians chant psalms, and the words of many Presbyterian hymns are translations of psalms in English meter. People in such churches are too familiar with the Bible way of praying to fall for the spurious counterfeit.

In conclusion, then, the positive confession movement exposes not only our greed and selfishness but our laziness in prayer and demand for instant self-gratification, even from God. It also exposes our ignorance of the Bible and our failure to use Jesus' teaching and the Psalms as the God-appointed models for our prayer life.

The success of the positive confession movement, in my view, highlights our need for repentance.

Appendix 2

Is Healing a Dangerous Fad?

This book differs from some similar works by stressing healing as a demonstration more of compassion than power, although the element of power is never far in the background. The issue of power in religion provokes controversy, with many feeling that an emphasis on power, including the power to heal, is a dangerous fad that diverts attention from the Gospel.

One book in particular levels this charge: *Power Religion: The Selling Out of the Evangelical Church?* (Moody Press, 1992). A symposium edited by Michael Scott Horton, it features chapters by many outstanding authors including Charles Colson, J. I. Packer, R. C. Sproul and James Montgomery Boice. The book focuses on several power emphases in the evangelical church, including the role of power in healing. Particular attention is given to the work of John Wimber, president of Vineyard Ministries International and the author (with Kevin Springer) of *Power Evangelism* (1986), *Power Healing* (1987) and *Power Points* (1991; all published by Harper & Row).

Anyone interested in healing evangelism should be aware of the objections raised in Horton's critique. In this appendix I want to look at those objections and respond.

Areas of Criticism

Horton writes that the goal of his symposium

> Is to point out what we believe to be serious distractions from the core mission and message of the Christian faith.
>
> page 15

> In short, this book is a warning about the uncritical adoption of paths to power that seem for a time to lead to greater spiritual vitality but in reality lead away from the One who is the Way, the Truth, and the Life.
>
> pages 19–20

Worldview

It criticizes Wimber and the Vineyard movement for the teaching that Western Christians need to undergo a "paradigm shift" away from their secular humanistic worldview. The book says,

> The Vineyard movement urges a major paradigm shift from rationalism to a more Eastern worldview.
>
> page 70

> But where are the disclaimers assuring us that this position does not mean the embrace of a pantheistic worldview?
>
> page 72

Many similar quotes assert that Wimber is calling us to embrace Eastern mysticism. I consider these warnings unfounded, since I find no reason to believe that Wimber is advocating an Eastern over a Western worldview, only that truth is to be found not in geography but in the Scriptures. He is calling us to a biblical worldview.

Power Evangelism and the Gospel

Two major criticisms are made of the relationship of Wimber's "power evangelism" and the Gospel. First, that the Gospel, as the saving message of the cross of Christ, is not clearly presented. Second, that a sensational emphasis on power demonstrations diverts attention from the message of the cross. The book says:

> One of the most significant things I noticed while reading Wimber's *Power Evangelism* was his failure to offer any definitions of the evangel (i.e., the gospel message).
>
> pages 80–81

> I am not claiming that Wimber and his associates are denying the essential articles of the gospel. Nevertheless, when the focus is on the unusual phenomena of signs and wonders rather than on the rational content of the gospel itself, confusion as to the main features of that message are bound to arise.
>
> page 81

> The signs and wonders movement shifts from the sublime to the ridiculous. It cheapens and overshadows the gospel.
>
> page 129

I consider these statements unfair. I have attended two lengthy seminars on power evangelism taught by Wimber and his staff, and have read Wimber's books.

His first two books, like the one I am writing, do not go into detail about the nature of the Gospel because they are written for those who already know what it is. Criticism that Wimber does not define the Gospel message carefully is like criticizing a book on advanced calculus for not including the multiplication tables! Wimber's third book, *Power Points*, does give some detail about the Gospel, and it is consistent with standard American evangelical theology.

While some things in the movement may be a bit sensational for my cold Calvinistic temperament, I find nothing that detracts from the Gospel of Jesus Christ.

Other Criticisms

There are other criticisms in Horton's symposium that should be noted briefly:

> Advanced courses in healing are offered, as though it were training in the magical arts.
>
> page 76

I consider this unfair and insulting. Wimber is teaching people to pray effectively for the sick. Courses in prayer are always appropriate. There is nothing in the content of these courses that compares with "magical arts." Somewhat acquainted with the arts of witch doctors in Uganda, I can assure you there is no comparison. Teaching reliance on the Holy Spirit is different from teaching the manipulation of evil spirits.

> Signs and wonders can be performed quite outside the heritage of the God of the Bible.
>
> page 94

This statement argues that since signs and wonders can be counterfeited by evil spirits, they cannot, therefore, convince people of Gospel truth.

People who know the counterfeit, however, need to see the greater power of Christ. It is precisely in those cultures where demonic signs and wonders are rampant that signs and wonders by the power of Christ are so important. It is those "outside the heritage of the God of the Bible" who need to see the power of the God of the Bible, or they will continue to fear their pagan deities.

> The signs and wonders movement has a realized eschatology in the sense that it considers any form of evangelism not accompanied by miracles as not being true evangelism.
>
> page 348

I question the fairness here. Some Christians in the Vineyard might regard evangelism as weak if there are never demonstrations of Christ's power, but weak is different from untrue.

Packer on Power

Perhaps the best (albeit indirect) response to Horton's symposium appears in a book by J. I. Packer, contributor to the symposium who did not contribute a chapter critical of healing. In this book, *Rediscovering Holiness* (Servant, 1992), Packer considers the issue of power more thoroughly. He writes:

> At the turn of each year *Time* magazine looks back, looks ahead, and makes whatever comments it thinks fit. The first issue for 1990 contained a list of "Buzzwords Most Ready for Early Retirement," in which . . . came "power player, power breakfast, power tie, power anything."
>
> As I look over my bookshelves today, I see there items titled *Power Healing, Power Evangelism, Healing Power, Power Encounters, When the Spirit Comes with Power, Christianity with Power,* all published since 1985. Round goes the wheels of my mind. Buzzword, eh? Fluffy, tiresome jargon, right? Overused among Christians just as it is in the commercial world? Ripe for retirement? First thoughts might prompt us to say so, but second thoughts should give us pause.
>
> For *power* is a very significant New Testament word. Where would I be if I imposed a self-denying ordinance on myself and declined to use it any longer? Where would the church be if we all acted that way? If we stopped talking about power we should soon stop thinking about it. If that happened we should be impoverished indeed. Hey, then, put on the brakes; stop being snide. For Christianity, at least, the word *power* is precious. Buzzword it may be, but we need it, so that we can focus on what it refers to.
>
> page 202

As he reflects, he thinks:

> More recently, Christians who have been touched by the movements known as Pentecostalism, the charismatic renewal, and the Third Wave have begun to seek (and some claim to have found) the ability through prayer to channel supernatural demonstrations of God's power in all sorts of healings: healings of the body, inner healings of the heart, and exorcisms where there appears to be something demonic acting in a person's life.
>
> Again I ask myself, is it wrong that Christians are concerned about these things? Though I see some dangerous pitfalls, I cannot find it in my heart to say this is wrong. In my New Testament, I read a good deal about such manifestations of the power of God, understood as "powers of the coming age" (Heb. 6:5)—in other words, the Holy Spirit in action.

> It is true that the New Testament regularly views the "signs and wonders" as the Father's authentication of the ministry of Jesus and his apostles (Acts 2:43, 5:12, 14:3, cf. 10:38, 19:11; Rom. 15:19; 2 Cor. 12:12; Heb. 2:4). There is no clear promise that these manifestations will continue after the apostles' ministry is over. But there is no denial that they will, either. The New Testament leaves open the possibility.
>
> pages 204–205

Further on he draws this conclusion:

> Thus, reflecting on the matter in the light of the New Testament, I am compelled to correct my initial feeling about *Time* magazine's wish to retire the word *power*. It remains a word in season for Christian people. Power is a theme that Christians must ever hold onto. It is very clear from the New Testament that the power of God is meant to accompany the gospel, and to find expression through its messengers and in the lives of those to whom the message comes.
>
> page 210

Having reached that conclusion, Packer then presents "five theses" about the manifestations of the power of God today. They are:

> 1. *Heightened Expectations.* It is right to bring the supernatural into prominence and to raise Christians' expectations with regard to it.
>
> page 212

> 2. *Empowered Ministry.* It is right to aspire to use one's God-given gifts in powerful and useful ministry.
>
> page 216

> 3. *Meeting Needs.* It is right to be a channel of divine power into other people's lives at their points of need.
>
> page 216

> 4. *Empowered Evangelism.* It is right to see God's power manifested in a way that has a significant evangelistic effect.
>
> page 218

> 5. *Real Righteousness.* It is right to be divinely empowered for righteousness, for moral victories, for deliverance from bad habits, for loving God and for pleasing God.
>
> page 219

My own interest in prayer for healing causes me to note what he says under his first thesis, which he calls "Packer's proverb." He writes:

> During the past thirty years openness to the supernatural in the physical realm has been recovered by many who had lost it. Expectations of divine healing and other startling providences in answer to prayer have risen throughout the Christian world. For this we should be thankful. Twentieth-century hostility to the idea that God might heal or shape events today in a way that would call attention to his presence in power was always unjustified and unbalanced. Its motives do not bear examination. We should be glad that it is melting away.
>
> page 214

Since Packer is one of the authors most admired by those who consider themselves "Truly Reformed," it is helpful in conclusion to see what he has to say about those intimations that charismatics call words of knowledge and that TRs denounce as "new special revelation." He writes:

> There are times—not many, but they do occur—when God gives great assurance as to what to pray for, and great confidence before the event that the prayer will be answered (as he did in Elijah's case). The memory of such occasions (one does not forget them!) remains as a strong incentive to pray confidently and expectantly about the next need that appears.
>
> I cannot claim to know much about this. But I recall a day of prayer for a Christian institution, for which I had some responsibility, that out of the blue had been told to close. Two hours into our praying I knew that I was being shown exactly what to ask for—a pattern of survival involving seven items. All of them at that moment seemed impossible to achieve, but all of them within eight months became reality. I recall, too, a morning when I walked home praying for a person facing a cancer operation the next day. As I neared home, the load of care lifted. I had a strange

> sense of being told I had been heard, and need not pray any more. Many others were praying for this person, and I do not know whether any of them had any such experience. All I know is that next day the surgeon could find no trace of cancer. Such precise intimations from God in advance as to how he plans to use his power are (I believe) very rare. But others have told similar stories of how God took them into his confidence, so to speak, while they were praying to him to use his power and show forth his glory in particular situations. As I said above, these things happen, and we should recognize and rejoice that they do.
>
> pages 231–232

Those of us engaged in healing evangelism are sure to be criticized, often unfairly. At the same time we need to realize that our ministries can become unbalanced and sensationalized, and guard against these dangers.

There are those who will try to identify us with positive confession teaching, and others who will object to any demonstration of power. And there are those who will object that our use of the power and gifts of the Holy Spirit is contrary to the tradition of the Protestant Reformation.

We will consider that objection in the third appendix.

Appendix 3

The Gifts and Guidance of the Spirit in the Reformed Tradition

The wife of a Presbyterian elder was diagnosed with terminal cancer. She sent her husband to the board of elders with a request that they come to the house and pray for her with the anointing of oil, according to James 5:14.

The elders debated her request. Some argued that the Scriptures required it and that they should therefore go. Others argued that it is not "Reformed." If the Reformers did not teach that this obligation is still in effect, why should we feel it necessary to conform?

But at the time of the Reformation, Europe was emerging from the Dark Ages. The Reformers had to sweep away centuries of traditional doctrine and practice that had no support in Scripture. At that time people associated James 5:14 with "extreme unction" or last rites. If the priest came to anoint you with oil, it was not so that you could be healed but so that you could die.

The Reformers felt they needed to wait until the medieval confusion had been removed from people's minds before they could restore the concept of oil for healing. Do away with extreme unction now. Institute oil for healing later.

Almost five centuries later Reformed Christians are still unwilling to anoint for healing, not because it is part of the Roman tradition but because it never became part of ours.

For six months the elders debated the matter of whether they should honor the request of the woman to be anointed with oil. Meanwhile, her cancer advanced and she declined rapidly. Finally, when she was close to death, they anointed her. Soon thereafter she went to heaven.

Many in the congregation regret to this day that the elders waited and debated so long. They believe that if the elders had responded promptly to her request, she might still be alive.

Tradition and (as in the above story) misunderstanding of tradition are hindrances to the Church's acceptance and use of healing evangelism.

All evangelicals are heirs of the Protestant Reformation. Many think the Reformers taught that all miracles and manifestational gifts ceased with the close of the apostolic age. They believe that the Reformers especially insisted that prophecy and gifts associated with revelation had necessarily ceased.

Many of the "Truly Reformed" (whom I mentioned in appendix 2) are convinced that people (like me) who believe that miracles and gifts continue are not Truly Reformed. They say we are fundamentally out of accord with the system of doctrine in Reformed churches and have no right to hold office in such churches.

The purpose of this appendix, then, is to consider the teachings of the Reformed tradition and see if there is a place in it for non-cessationists who practice healing evangelism.

The Reformers and Scriptural Sufficiency

Scriptural sufficiency was a central issue in the Reformation. Reformers pointed out that faith in Christ is the only condition of salvation taught in the Scriptures. The Roman Church replied that there were many conditions of salvation required by Church tradition. They said that God reveals Himself both in Scripture and in tradition, and they used tradition to support their arguments against the Reformers.

The Reformers responded that Scripture is sufficient and complete. God's self-revelation is limited to Scripture. When the canon of Scripture was closed, God had revealed everything He had to reveal. There would be no further revelation, not even in Church tradition.

Guidance

This conception of scriptural sufficiency is at the heart of Protestantism and is basic to the faith of all evangelicals, whether or not they are directly in the Reformed tradition.

We react with horror, therefore, at charismatics who talk of receiving "personal revelations" and having "revelational knowledge" in addition to scriptural revelation. This is why I stressed in chapter 10 that God speaks guidance for individuals and groups but not revelation. Revelation should be spoken of only in the technical sense used by the Westminster Confession of Faith, which speaks of revelation as being of that "which is necessary unto salvation" and of God Himself and His will for the Church.

I quote below the first article from the first chapter of the Confession and will refer to it again later:

> Although the light of nature, and the works of creation and providence, do so far manifest the goodness, wisdom and power of God, as to leave men inexcusable; yet they are not sufficient to give that knowledge of God and of his will, which is necessary unto salvation; therefore it pleased the Lord, at sundry times and in divers manners, to reveal himself, and to declare his will unto his Church; and afterwards, for the better preserving and propagating of the truth, and for the more sure establishment and comfort of the Church against the corruption of the flesh, and the malice of Satan and of the world, to commit the same wholly unto writing, which maketh the holy scripture to be the most necessary; these former ways of God's revealing his will unto his people being now ceased.

Manifestational Gifts

Closely related to the issue of whether God speaks guidance today is whether manifestational gifts exist today. Since these gifts are closely related to the operations of the Holy Spirit, those who insist that He does not speak to us today except through Scripture insist that therefore He does not give these gifts. They argue, moreover, that the purpose of the gifts was to authenticate the Gospel preached by the apostles as new revelation. Now that it is no longer brand-new, the authenticating gifts and miracles are no longer needed.

Some argue that the sole purpose of New Testament miracles was to authenticate the apostles. They base this teaching on 2 Corinthians 12:12: "The things that mark an apostle—-signs, wonders and miracles—were done among you with great perseverance."

Many scholars believe, however, that this verse is better translated in the King James: "Truly the signs of an apostle were wrought among you in all patience, in signs, and wonders, and mighty deeds." In this view, signs, wonders and miracles are not what mark apostleship but what accompany those marks. The marks of apostleship are the sufferings listed in the previous chapter, verses 22–33.

In any case, we know from the New Testament record that many who were not apostles also performed signs, wonders and miracles. If these were performed only by apostles, we might assume that they had ceased when the apostles were gone. Since other than apostles performed signs, wonders and miracles, is it not possible that others are doing so today?

The issue before us, however, is not whether signs and wonders may exist today, but whether those who teach that they exist today are teaching something contrary to the Reformed tradition.

The Reformers and Cessationism

It is often alleged that the Reformers taught not only scriptural sufficiency but that signs, wonders, manifestational gifts and miracles have all necessarily ceased. Those who believe that these signs continue, according to this view, stand in opposition to the teaching of the Reformers on an issue closely related to scriptural sufficiency.

At this point I must insist as a matter of historical fact that the Reformers did *not* teach that the gifts of the Spirit had ceased, even if they did not expect them to appear with the same frequency as I might expect them. If this is so—if they taught that the gifts may exist today—then I am not teaching contrary to the Reformers if I believe that they do exist today.

John Calvin

Many believe that John Calvin taught that gifts of the Holy Spirit, and especially prophecy, ceased with the close of the canon. That the gifts did cease is a common belief among Calvinists, but it was not Calvin's view. Calvin often spoke of the gifts being withdrawn due to unbelief, but he left open the possibility that they could be restored. Although he believed that the manifestation of gifts was rare, he did not believe that they were totally withdrawn in his own day.

Note the following quotations:

> Paul applies the name "prophets" not to all those who were interpreters of God's will, but to those who excelled in a particular revelation (Ephesians 4:11). This class either does not exist today or is less commonly seen.
>
> *Institutes*, 4:3:4, 2:1057

> It is not clear that he intended here [Romans 12:6] only those wonderful graces by which Christ adorned His Gospel at the beginning. We see rather that he is referring simply to ordinary gifts which remain perpetually in the Church.
>
> *Romans and Thessalonians*, page 269

And in a discussion of 1 Corinthians 12:28 and prophets:

> It is difficult to make up one's mind about gifts and offices of which the Church has been deprived for so long, except for mere traces or shades of them, which are still to be found.
>
> *First Corinthians*, page 271

John Knox and Samuel Rutherford

Although revelation ceased with the completion of the New Testament, non-revelational prophecies have continued in the Church, not only within fringe groups but among leaders of the Reformation. Some Reformed Christians say that the cessation of prophecies is a traditional Reformed doctrine—but in saying this they ignore their history.

John Knox, the disciple of John Calvin who became the father of Scottish Presbyterianism, was noted for his prophecies. Even the ultra-conservative Free Presbyterian Church of Scotland acknowledges Knox's gift.

In the biography entitled *Life of John Knox* (Free Presbyterian Church, 1960), author Thomas M'Crie tells of several prophecies:

> Of this kind were,
>
> • the assurance which he expressed from the beginning of the Scottish troubles, that the cause of the Congregation would ultimately prevail;
>
> • his confident hope of again preaching in his native country, and at St. Andrews, avowed by him during his imprisonment on board the French galleys, and frequently repeated during his exile;
>
> • with the intimations which he gave respecting the death of Thomas Maitland, and Kircaldy of Grange.
>
> It cannot be denied that his contemporaries considered these as proceeding from a prophetic spirit and have attested that they received an exact accomplishment.
>
> page 283

Samuel Rutherford, principal Scottish commissioner to the Westminster Assembly, a major theologian behind our Westminster Confession and a father of constitutional liberties by his book *Lex Rex*, believed that the gift of prophecy existed in his day and was manifested by Knox and other Reformers.

Rutherford's *Survey of the Spiritual Antichrist* says:

> There is a revelation of some particular men, who have foretold things to come even since the ceasing of the canon of the Word, as John Huss, Wycliffe, [and] Luther have foretold things to come, and they certainly fell out [came to pass].

> And in our own nation of Scotland, Mr. George Wishart foretold that Cardinal Beaton should not come out alive at the Castle of St. Andrews, but that he should die a shameful death, and he was hanged over the window that he did look out at, when he saw the man of God burnt.
>
> Mr. [John] Knox prophesied of the hanging of the Lord of Grange. Mr. John Davidson uttered prophecies, known to many of the kingdom. Diverse holy and mortified [sanctified] preachers in England have done the like.
>
> page 42 (quoted from an unpublished paper by Ron Lutjens)

How do modern Calvinists, those who believe that the gifts necessarily ceased, respond to the evidence that Calvin and others believed that they continued?

Kenneth Gentry writes in *The Charismatic Gift of Prophecy* (Footstool Publications, 1989):

> Calvin was at the very beginning of the Reformation and was rediscovering "lost" or obscured Biblical truths. As B. B. Warfield has commented: "We must bear in mind, on the one hand, that the young Calvin's book had practically no predecessors, but broke out a new path for itself. . . ."
>
> Calvin cannot be "discredited" for not holding to all the truths of which the Westminster Divines were aware in their more advanced stage of the progress of reformational doctrine.
>
> page 110

Apparently Gentry feels that the intervening centuries of theological reflection give him the right to say that Calvin was wrong and that those who agree with him are not Reformed. He is entitled to disagree with Calvin but not to say that a person is not an orthodox Calvinist who happens to agree with Calvin.

Arguments about Cessationism

Cessationism, the view that miracles necessarily ceased after the first century, became an article of orthodoxy only after it was taught by B. B. Warfield in 1918. He introduced the theory that miracles have necessarily ceased and will not reappear. He argued that the only purpose of miracles was to confirm the giving of new special revelation and that, since the Bible is complete, there can be no more miracles.

But confirming new special revelation is not the only purpose of miracles, as we saw in chapter 2. Jesus healed the sick because He had compassion on them (Matthew 9:35–36; 14:14; 20:34). Many miracles clustered around the ministries of Elijah and Elisha, who were not giving new revelation but bearing witness to the old revelation of the supremacy of Yahweh. And the miracles that confirmed the message in the New Testament may have been doing so not because it was new revelation but because it is the eternal Gospel.

Strict cessationists believe that men and women who believe as I do are fundamentally out of accord with the system of doctrine of the Reformed churches and should be defrocked. They base this argument on their interpretation of the Westminster Confession of Faith that teaches that even as revelation has ceased, so the means of communicating revelation have ceased.

The first article of the first chapter of the Confession (quoted in full above) states that "it pleased the Lord, at sundry times, and in divers manners, to reveal himself, and to declare his will unto his Church." Then it states that He was pleased "to commit the same wholly unto writing, which maketh the holy scripture to be the most necessary; those former ways of God's revealing his will unto his people being now ceased."

The Confession is telling us that first God revealed Himself and then He committed that revelation to writing. It tells us that the written Scriptures are necessary because God is no longer revealing Himself as He did in the past.

Cessationists use the phrase *those former ways of God's revealing his will unto his people being now ceased* to argue that non-cessationists teach contrary to the Confession and should be removed from church office. It is argued that because we believe God speaks guidance to His people through prophecies, words of knowledge, words of wisdom, etc., therefore we do not believe that those ways of revelation have ceased, and are teaching contrary to the Confession.

But consider dreams, one of the ways God communicated in Bible times. Have dreams ceased? Of course not. People continue to dream. But dreams have ceased as media of communicating new revelation. That is all the Confession is teaching here. Since revelation has ceased, the means that were used for the communication of revelation have ceased to be means for communicating revelation.

Cessationists respond by citing Article Two of the Confession. It lists the books in the canon and then says, "All which are given by inspiration of God, to be the rule of faith and life."

Gentry says in *The Charismatic Gift of Prophecy*:

> Alluded to here are not just doctrinal-redemptive matters (i.e., matters of "faith"), but also matters of all of "life." We do not need another voice from God; He has given us His Word to direct us in life.
>
> page 120

If the Scripture teaches us everything necessary for life (Gentry is saying), then we do not receive guidance from the Holy Spirit. If we did receive guidance from the Spirit, then the Scriptures would not be sufficient in matters of life. That is the cessationist argument.

Let me address this argument.

It is common in the Reformed tradition to talk about faith and life. By faith we are referring to doctrine; by life we are referring to practice. A common statement is, "The Bible is the infallible rule of faith and life." That is, not only is the Bible true when it teaches us doctrine, but it is true when it instructs us about living the Christian life. It is true in practical as well as theological matters.

When the Westminster Confession tells us that the Bible is sufficient in matters of life, it is telling us that the Bible gives all the information necessary for every Christian to live the Christian life. We need neither Church tradition nor modern prophets to give us further instruction on morals and sacraments.

But to say that the Scriptures are complete in telling everything that every Christian needs to know to live the Christian life is not to deny that the Holy Spirit often gives guidance in individual matters. Scripture teaches everything every Christian needs to know. But it does not tell a specific individual where to live, whom to marry, what he should do for a career or how he should devote his time on a particular day. These things do not fall into the scope of Scripture nor should they be dictated by the Church. They are matters for the leading of the Spirit.

That there is no guidance by the Holy Spirit for believers today is a necessary consequence of the views of cessationists. Most Christians are not going to buy their rationalistic theory. Most of us know what it is to be led by the Holy Spirit. And our confidence in divine guidance is in no way a violation of our deep commitment to the sufficiency of Scripture.

I believe that revelation has ceased and that the means of revelation have ceased as means of revelation. I also agree with the Reformers that the guidance and gifts of the Holy Spirit may and do continue. I reject the cessationism of Warfield and believe Reformed orthodoxy began with the Reformers, not in 1918. Those who insist that non-cessationists should be put out of the church are insisting on a very recent tradition.

Appendix 4

Resources

Here are organizations you may turn to for additional resources. The first kind of organization is the renewal service committee that serves specific denominational traditions. You should start by contacting the committee related to your denomination. The second kind is the organization offering resources specifically on healing and/or prayer to Christians from many traditions. Whenever possible I give the name of the executive director.

When contacting these organizations, it is helpful to enclose a contribution. That way you can be confident that they will put you on their mailing list and you will be helping them in their work.

Renewal Service Committees, by Tradition

All traditions (a coalition of many renewal service committees)

The Rev. Dr. Vinson Synan
North American Renewal
Services Committee
P.O. Box 1056
Chesapeake, VA 23320

American Baptist
The Rev. Gary K. Clark
American Baptist
Charismatic Fellowship
1386 N. Sierra Bonita Ave.
Pasadena, CA 91104-2647

Anabaptist/Mennonite
The Rev. Doug Fike
Empowered Ministries
P.O. Box 9
Warm Springs, VA 24484

Episcopal
The Rev. Charles B. Fulton, Jr.
Episcopal Renewal Ministries
1341 Terrell Mill Rd., Ste 130
Marietta, GA 30067

Lutheran
The Rev. Larry Christenson
International Lutheran Renewal Center
2701 Rice St.
St. Paul, MN 55113-2200

Lutheran, Missouri Synod
The Rev. Del Rossin
Renewal in Missouri
1727 Kaneville Rd.
Geneva, IL 60134

Methodist
Mr. Gary Moore
United Methodist Renewal Service
P.O. Box 1205
Goodlettsville, TN 37070

Presbyterian & Reformed
The Rev. Dr. Brad Long
Presbyterian & Reformed Renewal Ministries International
P.O. Box 429
Black Mountain, NC 28711

United Church of Christ
The Rev. Vernon Stoop
Focus Renewal Ministries
P.O. Box 330
Sassamansville, PA 19472

Organizations on Healing or Prayer

Healing

The Rev. Francis MacNutt
Christian Healing Ministries, Inc.
P.O. Box 9520
Jacksonville, FL 32208

The Rev. Canon Mark Pearson
Institute for Christian Renewal
148 Plaistow Rd.
Plaistow, NH 03865

Anne S. White
Victorious Ministry through Christ
P. O. Box 1804
Winter Park, FL 32790

Dr. William Wilson
Institute of Christian Growth
P.O. Box 2347
Burlington, NC 27216

Bill and Delores Winder
Fellowship Foundation
P.O. Box 9345
Shreveport, LA 71139

Prayer

The Rev. Ray Bringham
Prayer Summit
1299 Deer Springs Rd.
San Marcos, CA 92069

The Rev. David Bryant
Concerts of Prayer
P.O. Box 36008
Minneapolis, MN 55435

Cindy Jacobs
Generals of Intercession
P.O. Box 49788
Colorado Springs, CO 80949-9788

The Rev. Dr. C. Peter Wagner
Global Harvest Ministries
215 N. Marengo Ave., Ste 151
Pasadena, CA 91101

For more information on the ministry of Don Dunkerley, please write to:

The Rev. Don Dunkerley
P.O. Box 335
Pensacola, FL 32592

Phone: (904) 438-1267

Bibliography

Suggested Reading

Here are books that I find among the most valuable on several basic topics. I have divided them by category and included comments about a few of them. Following this listing are books that were cited in the text of *Healing Evangelism.*

Prayer

Bounds, E. M. *The Complete Works of E. M. Bounds on Prayer.* Grand Rapids: Baker, 1990, 568 pp.

Cho, Paul [David] Yonggi. *Prayer: Key to Revival.* Waco, Tex.: Word, 1984, 177 pp.

Dawson, John. *Taking Our Cities for God: How to Break Spiritual Strongholds.* Altamonte Springs, Fla.: Creation House, 1989, 219 pp.

Duewel, Wesley L. *Mighty Prevailing Prayer.* Grand Rapids: Zondervan, 1990, 332 pp. Outstanding!

Eastman, Dick. *Love on Its Knees: Make a Difference by Praying for Others.* Grand Rapids: Chosen, 1989, 187 pp.

Hallesby, O. *Prayer*. Minneapolis: Augsburg, 1959, 176 pp. A classic!

Jacobs, Cindy. *Possessing the Gates of the Enemy: A Training Manual for Militant Intercession*. Grand Rapids: Chosen, 1991, 249 pp.

Kelly, Douglas F. *If God Already Knows, Why Pray?* Brentwood, Tenn.: Wolgemuth & Hyatt, 1989, 217 pp.

Lea, Larry. *Could You Not Tarry One Hour?* Altamonte Springs, Fla.: Creation House, 1987, 191 pp.

Murray, Andrew. *With Christ in the School of Prayer*. Westwood, N.J.: Barbour & Company, 1986, 274 pp. A classic and a staple in my own ministerial training.

Pratt, Richard. *Pray with Your Eyes Open*. Phillipsburg, N.J.: Presbyterian & Reformed, 1987, 193 pp.

Torrey, R. A. *Power and Peace in Prayer*. Westchester, Ill.: Good News, 1978, 63 pp.

Wagner, C. Peter. *Breaking Strongholds in Your City*. Ventura, Calif.: Regal, 1993, 232 pp.

Wagner, C. Peter. *Churches that Pray*. Ventura, Calif.: Regal, 1993, 226 pp.

Wagner, C. Peter, *Prayer Shield*. Ventura, Calif.: Regal, 1992, 197 pp.

Wagner, C. Peter. *Warfare Prayer*. Ventura, Calif.: Regal, 1992, 197 pp.

The Holy Spirit

Christenson, Larry, ed. *Welcome, Holy Spirit*. Minneapolis: Augsburg, 1987, 418 pp.

Christenson, Larry. *Speaking in Tongues and Its Significance for the Church*. Minneapolis: Dimension Books, 1971, 141 pp.

Deere, Jack. *Surprised by the Power of the Spirit*. Grand Rapids: Zondervan, 1993, 292 pp.

Eaton, Michael A. *Baptism with the Spirit: The Teaching of Martyn Lloyd-Jones*. London: InterVarsity, 1989, 253 pp. Shows that Lloyd-Jones has correctly interpreted and presented the Puritan view of Spirit baptism as a work of assurance subsequent to regeneration.

Graves, Robert W. *Praying in the Spirit*. Grand Rapids: Chosen, 1987, 159 pp.

Grudem, Wayne. *The Gift of Prophecy in the New Testament and Today*. Westchester, Ill.: Crossway, 1988, 337 pp.

Hummel, Charles E. *Fire in the Fireplace*. Downers Grove, Ill.: InterVarsity, 1993, 308 pp.

Lederle, Henry I. *Treasures Old and New*. Peabody, Mass.: Hendrickson, 1988, 262 pp. A survey of many views of Spirit baptism. The section on the Puritans shows that they viewed it as a work of assurance subsequent to regeneration.

Lloyd-Jones, Martyn. *Joy Unspeakable: Power and Renewal in the Holy Spirit*. Wheaton, Ill.: Harold Shaw, 1984, 280 pp.

Lloyd-Jones, Martyn. *Revival*. Westchester, Ill.: Crossway, 1987, 316 pp. Indicates that revival is often accompanied by the outpouring of spiritual gifts, especially prophecy.

Lloyd-Jones, Martyn. *The Sovereign Spirit: Discerning His Gifts*. Wheaton, Ill.: Harold Shaw, 1985. Part 2 of the sermon series of which *Joy Unspeakable* was part 1. Argues that the gifts of the Spirit are still being sovereignly distributed today.

Packer, J. I. *Keep in Step with the Spirit*. Grand Rapids: Revell, 1984, 285 pp. An excellent and fair work by a non-charismatic.

Sherrill, John L. *They Speak with Other Tongues*. Grand Rapids: Chosen, 1985, 171 pp.

Torrey, R. A. *The Holy Spirit*. Grand Rapids: Revell, 1927, 201 pp. A classic, recommended to me by Lloyd-Jones.

Worldview

Kraft, Charles H. *Christianity with Power*. Ann Arbor: Servant, 1989, 212 pp. This is an extremely important work! You don't want to miss it.

Lewis, Clive Staples. *The Screwtape Letters*. London: Centenary Press, 1942, 160 pp.

Long, Zeb Bradford and Douglas McMurry. *The Collapse of the Brass Heaven: Rebuilding Our Worldview to Embrace the Power of God*. Grand Rapids: Chosen, 1994, 267 pp.

Springer, Kevin, ed. *Power Encounters Among Christians in the*

Western World. San Francisco: Harper & Row, 1988, 218 pp.

Wagner, C. Peter. *The Third Wave of the Holy Spirit*. Ann Arbor: Servant, 1988, 130 pp.

Wagner, C. Peter, ed. *Signs and Wonders Today*. Altamonte Springs, Fla.: Creation House, 1987, 158 pp.

White, John. *When the Spirit Comes with Power*. Downers Grove, Ill.: InterVarsity, 1988, 246 pp.

Williams, Don. *Signs, Wonders and the Kingdom of God*. Ann Arbor: Servant, 1989, 152 pp.

Healing

Blue, Ken. *Authority to Heal*. Downers Grove, Ill.: InterVarsity, 1987, 168 pp.

MacNutt, Francis. *Healing*. Altamonte Springs, Fla.: Creation House, 1988, 333 pp. A classic!

MacNutt, Francis. *Overcome by the Spirit*. Grand Rapids: Chosen, 1990, 188 pp. The healing effects of resting in the Spirit.

MacNutt, Francis. *The Power to Heal*. Notre Dame, Ind.: Ave Maria Press, 1985, 254 pp.

MacNutt, Francis. *The Prayer that Heals*. Notre Dame, Ind.: Ave Maria Press, 1981, 116 pp.

Pearson, Mark A. *Christian Healing: A Practical, Comprehensive Guide, 2nd Edition*. Grand Rapids: Chosen, 1995, 308 pp.

Sanford, Agnes. *Behold Your God*. St. Paul: Macalester Park, 1989, 201 pp.

Sanford, Agnes. *The Healing Light*. New York: Ballantine, 1972, 174 pp.

Wagner, C. Peter. *How to Have a Healing Ministry in Any Church*. Ventura, Calif.: Regal, 1988, 269 pp.

Whitaker, Bob, and Doug McMurry. *Equipping for Congregational Renewal*. A retreat syllabus circulated privately by Presbyterian & Reformed Renewal Ministries International, Black Mountain, N.C., n.d.

Wimber, John with Kevin Springer. *Power Evangelism*. San Francisco: Harper & Row, 1986, 201 pp.

Wimber, John with Kevin Springer. *Power Healing*. San Francisco: Harper & Row, 1987, 293 pp.

Wimber, John with Kevin Springer. *Power Points*. San Francisco: Harper & Row, 1991, 208 pp.

Winder, Delores with Bill Keith. *Jesus Set Me Free*. Shreveport, La.: Fellowship Foundation, 1986, 106 pp. Chronicles Delores' amazing healing.

Zuendell, Frederick. *Pastor Blumhardt*. Newton, Kan.: Herald of His Coming, 1993, 16 pp.

Counseling and Deliverance

Anderson, Neil T. *The Bondage Breaker*. Eugene, Ore.: Harvest House, 1990, 249 pp.

Anderson, Neil T. *Victory over the Darkness*. Ventura, Calif.: Regal, 1990, 245 pp.

Bubeck, Mark I. *Overcoming the Adversary*. Chicago: Moody, 1984, 139 pp.

Harper, Michael. *Spiritual Warfare*. Ann Arbor: Servant, 1984, 109 pp.

Kraft, Charles H. *Defeating Dark Angels*. Ann Arbor: Servant, 1992, 250 pp.

Sandford, John and Paula. *Healing the Wounded Spirit*. Tulsa: Victory House, 1985, 473 pp.

Sandford, John and Paula. *The Transformation of the Inner Man*. Tulsa: Victory House, 1982, 412 pp.

Sandford, John and Mark. *A Comprehensive Guide to Deliverance and Inner Healing*. Grand Rapids: Chosen, 1992, 383 pp.

Wagner, C. Peter, ed. *Territorial Spirits*. Chichester, England: Sovereign World, 1991, 202 pp.

Wagner, C. Peter, and F. Douglas Pennoyer, eds. *Wrestling with Dark Angels*. Ventura, Calif.: Regal, 1990, 357 pp.

Reformed Classics

Calvin, John. *First Corinthians*. Edinburgh: Oliver & Boyd, 1960, 358 pp.

Calvin, John. *Institutes of the Christian Religion*. Louisville: Westminster, 1960. In two volumes.

Calvin, John. *Romans and Thessalonians*. Grand Rapids: Eerdmans, 1961, 423 pp.

M'Crie, Thomas. *The Life of John Knox*. Inverness, Scotland: Free Presbyterian Church of Scotland, 1960, 290 pp.

[Westminster] Confession of Faith, The. Inverness, Scotland: Publications Committee of the Free Presbyterian Church of Scotland, 1976, 422 pp.

Other Materials

In addition to some of the books above, the following were cited in the text of *Healing Evangelism*:

Gentry, Kenneth. *The Charismatic Gift of Prophecy*. Memphis: Footstool, 1989, 144 pp.

Greenway, Roger S. "Sickness, Prayer, and Healing." *Missionary Monthly*, January 1993, Vol. 99B.

Horton, Michael S., ed. *Power Religion*. Chicago: Moody, 1992, 353 pp. Responded to in appendix 2.

McConnell, D. R. *A Different Gospel*. Peabody, Mass.: Hendrickson, 1988, 195 pp. An important work for understanding the positive confession movement. It is especially strong on the origins of the doctrine.

McDonnell, Kilian, and George T. Montague. *Christian Initiation and Baptism in the Holy Spirit*. Collegeville, Minn.: The Liturgical Press, 1991, 342 pp.

Packer, J. I. *Rediscovering Holiness*. Ann Arbor: Servant, 1992, 276 pp. Quoted extensively in appendix 2.

Sayer, George. *Jack: A Life of C. S. Lewis*. Wheaton, Ill.: Crossway, 1994, 450 pp.